WARRIORS OF THE CROSS

Merlin L. Neff

Pacific Press® Publishing Association
Nampa, Idaho
Oshawa, Ontario, Canada
www.pacificpress.com

Cover design by Gerald Lee Monks
Cover illustration by Clyde Provonsha
Inside design by Steve Lanto

All Scriptures quoted are from The New King James Version,
copyright © 1979, 1980, 1982, Thomas Nelson, Inc., Publishers.

Library of Congress Cataloging-in-Publication Data

Neff, Merlin L.
Warriors of the Cross / Merlin L. Neff.
p. cm. — (Champions of faith ; v. 5)
ISBN 13: 978-0-8163-2268-8 (hard cover)
ISBN 10: 0-8163-2268-6
1. Bible stories, English—N.T. I. Title.
BS2401.N44 2008
225.9'505—dc22
2008007998

Additional copies of this book are available by calling toll-free
1-800-765-6955 or by visiting http://www.adventistbookcenter.com.

08 09 10 11 12 • 5 4 3 2 1

"Train up a child in the way he should go, and when he is old he will not depart from it."

—Proverbs 22:6

Interior Illustrations:

Norman Brice: pages 29, 92.
Lars Justinen: page 64.
Joe Maniscalco: pages 16, 39.
Heber Pintos: page 108.
Clyde Provonsha: pages 1, 36, 37.
John Steel: pages 8, 12, 20, 21, 25, 44, 45, 49, 53, 57, 61, 68, 72, 73, 76, 80, 88, 96, 100, 105, 113, 117, 120, 125, 128, 130, 136, 137, 140, 141, 145.
O. Stemler: page 85.
Sheldon Van Etten: page 144.

CONTENTS

FOR PARENTS

**Pass Your Values On to Your Children
Through Bible Stories**

As a parent, you likely want your nine- or ten- or eleven-year-old daughter or son to enter the teen years knowing the most important stories of the Bible. As you look for ways to pass on to your child the love of God and the principles that represent His character, consider how well a good story captures the attention of human beings of all ages. The Bible stories in these five volumes will place God's principles in your child's mind in such a way that they won't forget them as they grow older.

Read these books with your child—or have the child read the story to you—morning or evening or Sabbath afternoon, every week. This is a good way to build your child's character and faith in God without your having to explain a bunch of abstract ideas. Their awareness of how God works with His people will grow without them realizing it.

Every generation through history that forgot about the Scriptures, and therefore the knowledge and implementation of God's principles, has suffered greatly from its own evil and self-destructive actions. A similar destiny awaits the children of this generation if we fail to bring the stories of the Bible to bear on their lives. The stakes are too high, the dangers too close, for us to neglect the story of salvation as we raise our children.

The timeless truths of the Bible come through clearly in the stories of this five-volume set. Each story has been screened for some elements more suited to adult readers. The stories chosen are the ones that follow the thread of salvation down through the centuries. In places where people of the Bible speak to each other, the words are quoted from the New King James Version, which is fairly easy to understand and widely accepted.

Pray for your child that he or she will respond positively when the Holy Spirit speaks to his or her heart. These Bible stories may bring your child to a turning point of knowing God in their own experience and accepting His love and His principles for themselves. There is supernatural power in the Word of God that may change your son or daughter forever.

The Publisher

MEN OF GREAT POWER

Acts 1:9–2:47

The eleven disciples of Jesus stood on the Mount of Olives, stunned by what they had seen and heard.

For three and a half years they had loved their Master and followed Him wherever He went. They had been with Him when He fed the hungry thousands. They had stood at His side when He healed the sick and raised the dead. They had been near the cross when He was put to death by Roman soldiers. And they knew that on the third day afterward, He had come out of the tomb as the Mighty Prince, Conqueror of death.

Forty days had passed since Jesus left the tomb, and on this day He had taken His disciples to the Mount of Olives. They went out through the gate of the city, up the path near the Garden of Gethsemane, and on to the mountain overlooking Jerusalem. There, Jesus told His disciples that He must go back to His Father in heaven. He also promised, "I will come again."

Jesus talked to His disciples about their future work.

He said, "You shall receive power when the Holy Spirit has come upon you; and you shall be witnesses to Me in Jerusalem, and in all Judea and Samaria, and to the end of the earth."

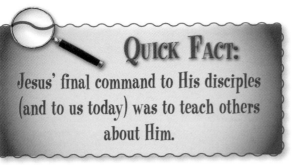

QUICK FACT:
Jesus' final command to His disciples (and to us today) was to teach others about Him.

While Jesus was speaking to His closest friends, He rose up from the earth. Slowly He ascended, and then a cloud hid Him from their view.

The amazed men stood gazing upward to catch a last glimpse of their Lord. When they looked around, they saw two heavenly messengers in white robes standing by them. One of the messengers said, "Men of Galilee, why do you stand gazing up into heaven? This same Jesus, who was taken up from you into heaven, will so come in like manner as you saw Him go into heaven."

The eleven followers of the Mighty Prince wondered what they should do. How could they be witnesses? Where should they go? Jesus had told them to wait in Jerusalem, so they left the Mount of Olives and hiked down the path toward the city. As they went in through the city gate, they began to talk excitedly, and a new light gleamed in their eyes. They would tell others about Jesus the Messiah. They would repeat His promise, "I will come again."

Peter was no longer interested in fishing. He must tell the people of Jerusalem about his Master. James and John no longer dreamed of the most important offices in the kingdom. They were ready to tell everyone they met about the risen Savior. Matthew would never return to the tax collector's desk. He knew that he must spend the rest of his life in the service of the Man from Nazareth.

The disciples went to the upstairs room where they had been staying. Kneeling down in prayer, they asked God to help them tell the story of Jesus. Over the next few days they planned how they might carry out the Master's command to give His message to the whole world.

Then one day Peter reminded the group that Judas, the betrayer, was dead. It was time to choose another man to take his place. Peter suggested that one of the men who had been associated with them since the time Jesus was baptized should be chosen to complete the group of twelve.

The names of Joseph and Matthias were proposed. Once more the disciples knelt in prayer. Then they drew names, and Matthias was chosen as the twelfth member of the group. We now call these men apostles, which means "men who are sent." However, before they could be sent, they had to be sure of their message. The followers of Jesus stayed in Jerusalem, waiting for the power from heaven to prepare them for their work.

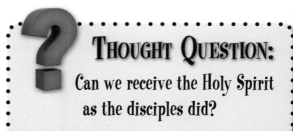

THOUGHT QUESTION: Can we receive the Holy Spirit as the disciples did?

The Day of Pentecost, or the harvest festival, came fifty days after the Passover Feast. This was the festival when the people of Israel brought the first fruits of their orchards and fields to God's house. The city was filled with pilgrims who had come for the thanksgiving celebration.

The apostles were staying in the same upstairs room on the Day of Pentecost. They gathered in a circle and prayed. Suddenly they heard a loud roar like a rushing mighty wind. God's Spirit had come to them. A glorious light like tongues of flame appeared above the head of each apostle. They were all filled with the Holy Spirit. And the apostles began to speak in different foreign languages!

Jews from many countries had come to this Feast of Pentecost. When they heard the sound like a big wind, they were curious and excited. The visitors gathered in a crowd to hear the words spoken by men who had followed Jesus. Jews from faraway Media, Mesopotamia, Egypt, Rome, and Arabia heard the story of the Messiah in their own language!

"Whatever could this mean?" one person called out.

Others, mocking the disciples, said, "They are full of new wine."

Peter began to address the large crowd, while his eleven companions gathered around him. He explained, "Men of Judea and all who dwell in Jerusalem, let this be known to you, and heed my words. For these are not drunk, as you suppose, since it is only the third hour of the day." Jews did not partake of food or drink before nine in the morning, because it was the hour of prayer. Furthermore, they ate nothing before noon on feast days.

Peter reminded his listeners about the prophecies of Joel and David concerning the Messiah. He told them that the hope of Israel had come. "This Jesus God has raised up," he said, "of which we are all witnesses. Therefore being exalted to the right hand of God, and having received from the Father the promise of the Holy Spirit, He poured out this which you now see and hear."

He went on to say, "Therefore let all the house of Israel know assuredly that God has made this Jesus, whom you crucified, both Lord and Christ."

When the people heard these words they were stung in their hearts, and they asked the disciples, "Men and brethren, what shall we do?"

"Repent," said Peter, "and let every one of you be baptized in the name of Jesus Christ for the remission of sins."

As a result of Peter's message, many were baptized. About three thousand people joined the apostles that day. In this way, the number of followers of Jesus grew rapidly. Soon there was a large church of faithful believers. Each day the members went to the temple to worship. They were happy to obey God's Word and to follow the teachings of the risen Savior.

GOD SAYS:

" 'Repent, and let every one of you be baptized in the name of Jesus Christ for the remission of sins; and you shall receive the gift of the Holy Spirit.' " -Acts 2:38

The Jewish leaders in Jerusalem had thought their troubles were over when they crucified Jesus. Now His disciples were causing great excitement in the city. Thousands of people were flocking to them.

Because of this, the priests and rulers became angry and plotted how they would stop these men. They decided to give them a good scare that would cause them to leave Jerusalem. If necessary they would threaten them with death. They remembered how the disciples who had been with Jesus in the Garden of Gethsemane had run away the night He was betrayed. The Jewish leaders did not yet know about the wonderful power that had filled the hearts of the apostles. The disciples now had courage and strength to stand for their Leader, the Mighty Prince.

PETER AND JOHN IN JAIL

Acts 3; 4

One afternoon as the apostles Peter and John were on their way up to the temple for the 3:00 P.M. hour of prayer, they saw a crippled man. He was being carried on a stretcher by his friends to his usual place by the Beautiful Gate. He was more than forty years old, and every day he would beg from the people who came to worship in the temple. When this beggar, who had been crippled from birth, saw Peter and John, he stretched out his hands and asked for a gift of money.

Peter looked intently at the man and said, "Look at us!"

Instantly the man gave them his full attention, supposing that he would receive some coins. But Peter said, "Silver and gold I do not have, but what I do have I give you."

The beggar sank back on his pallet, and a shadow of disappointment crossed his face. Then he heard Peter say, "In the name of Jesus Christ of Nazareth, rise up and walk."

The apostle took the crippled man by the right hand and lifted him up. Immediately his legs and ankles became strong. For the first time in his life, he sprang forward and began to walk around. He walked with the apostles into the temple court. The crowds of people in the court saw the crippled man who had been at the Beautiful Gate for so many years. He was walking, leaping, and shouting praises to God! The people were astonished. Some began to say that the power to work miracles had been given to the followers of Jesus of Nazareth.

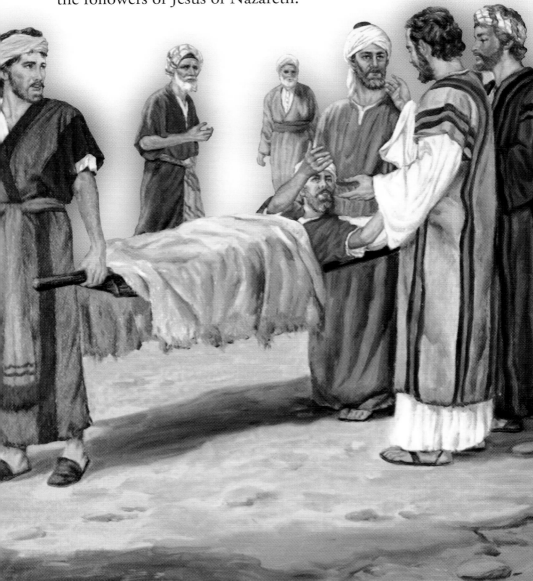

The excited beggar held on to Peter and John as the men in the temple crowded around them. Seeing the shocked stares of the people, Peter said, "Men of Israel, why do you marvel at this? Or why look so intently at us, as though by our own power or godliness we had made this man walk?" Then he went on to tell them about Jesus. "You denied the Holy One and the Just, and asked for a murderer to be granted to you, and killed the Prince of life, whom God raised from the dead, of which we are witnesses. And His name, through faith in His name, has made this man strong, whom you see and know. Yes, the faith which comes through Him has given him this perfect soundness in the presence of you all."

Thought Question: Why was it important for the people to understand that it wasn't by Peter's power that the lame man was healed?

Then, in a kind voice, Peter said, "Yet now, brethren, I know that you did it in ignorance, as did also your rulers."

While Peter was addressing the people, the high priests and other leaders pushed their way through the crowd. They commanded the temple guards to arrest Peter and John. Since it was already evening, it was too late to have a trial. They put the two apostles in jail until the next morning. But the spread of the story of Jesus could not be stopped. Many who had heard Peter's message believed it, and the church grew to about five thousand members.

The next morning the leaders met in council with An-nas, the high priest, and Caiaphas. They sent for the apostles and had them brought in to answer questions about the crippled man. The leaders hoped to frighten Peter and John so that they would stop telling the story of Jesus.

"By what power or by what name have you done this?" the leaders asked.

Peter and John faced their enemies without fear. The beggar whom they had healed stood next to them. Filled with the Holy Spirit of God, Peter said to the council members, "Rulers of the people and elders of Israel: If we this day are judged for a good deed done to a helpless man, by what means he has been made well, let it be known to you all, and to all the people of Israel, that by the name of Jesus Christ of Nazareth, whom you crucified, whom God raised from the dead, by Him this man stands here before you whole."

The Jewish leaders looked at one another in amazement. Peter was obviously not an educated man, but he was speaking boldly and clearly. They realized that the two apostles had been with Jesus. Since the healed beggar was standing in front of them, they could say nothing in response. Peter continued to speak. "Nor is there salvation in any other, for there is no other name under heaven given among men by which we must be saved."

GOD SAYS:

" 'Repent therefore and be converted, that your sins may be blotted out.' " –Acts 3:19

A few weeks earlier, Annas and Caiaphas had helped put Jesus to death; and now the apostle was saying that this Man of Nazareth could save the world. It was astounding! The leaders commanded that Peter, John, and the beggar be held outside the courtroom so that they could confer among themselves.

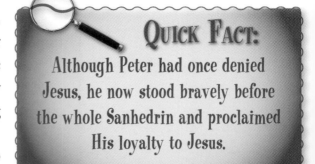

QUICK FACT:
Although Peter had once denied Jesus, he now stood bravely before the whole Sanhedrin and proclaimed His loyalty to Jesus.

"What shall we do to these men?" was the first question, as the council members looked at one another. They knew that a man who had been a helpless cripple for years was now strong and well. How could they oppose such a miracle? Many people in Jerusalem had seen the healed man with their own eyes.

Then one of them said, "But so that it spreads no further among the people, let us severely threaten them, that from now on they speak to no man in this name."

They called Peter and John before them and told them that they must not tell the story of Jesus ever again.

Peter did not turn tail when he heard the verdict. He said, "Whether it is right in the sight of God to listen to you more than to God, you judge. For we cannot but speak the things which we have seen and heard."

The leaders threatened them again, but they were afraid to punish the men because so many people had seen the miracle. Peter and John went back to their church members and told all that had happened. Then they had a prayer meeting, thanking God for His protection and blessing.

As new members came into the church, they were loved and cared for by the believers. The poor in the church received enough money and food to supply their needs. No one among them went without, because each of the members shared what he had.

STEPHEN, THE FIRST MARTYR

Acts 5–7

Among the church members who sold property was Barnabas, who brought the money and gave it to the apostles. Another man named Ananias also sold his property, but he kept back part of the money. When Ananias came in and said that he was giving all the money from the sale of his property, Peter could tell that he was not telling the truth.

"Ananias, why has Satan filled your heart to lie to the Holy Spirit and keep back part of the price of the land for yourself?" Peter asked. "While it remained, was it not your own? And after it was sold, was it not in your own control? Why have you conceived this thing in your heart? You have not lied to men but to God."

When Ananias heard this, he fell to the ground and died. The people nearby became afraid. Some young men in the room wrapped up the body of the dead man, carried it to the graveyard, and buried it.

About three hours later, Sapphira, the wife of Ananias, came to see Peter. She did not know what had happened to her husband. The apostle said to her, "Tell me whether you sold the land for so much?"

"Yes," she said, "for so much." Sapphira, too, was telling a lie when she said this.

"How is it that you have agreed together to test the Spirit of the Lord?" Peter asked. "Look, the feet of those who have buried your husband are at the door, and they will carry you out."

Instantly Sapphira fell down and died. The young men carried out her body and buried it beside the body of her husband. Word of these deaths spread among the believers.

THOUGHT QUESTION:
Why were Sapphira and Ananias punished so severely for their lie?

Many miracles took place through the work of the apostles. The sick were brought into the street so that when Peter passed, his shadow could fall on them and they might be healed. All the people of Jerusalem were talking about the wonderful happenings. Crowds flocked from the nearby towns, bringing their sick friends and relatives with them. They were all healed.

The high priests and other leaders became jealous of the honor and power that had been given to the apostles. Once again they arrested the apostles and put them in the common prison. That night an angel of the Lord opened the door of the prison and let them out. "Go, stand in the temple and speak to the people all the words of this life," the angel told them.

The next day the acting high priest and his counselors came together to decide how they would punish the prisoners. The apostles were sent for, but the officials who went to the prison came back with bad news. "Indeed we found the prison shut securely, and the guards standing outside before the doors," said the men, "but when we opened them, we found no one inside!"

QUICK FACT:
God's laws are more important than the laws of man.

About this time a messenger came running in to the council and said, "Look, the men whom you put in prison are standing in the temple and teaching the people!"

The leaders sent a captain and his officers to bring the apostles back for more questioning. The officers brought them out of the temple carefully, because they did not want to be stoned by the people.

When the disciples stood before the high priest, he said to them, "Did we not strictly command you not to teach in this name? And look, you have filled Jerusalem with your doctrine, and intend to bring this Man's blood on us!"

"We ought to obey God rather than men," said fearless Peter. "The God of our fathers raised up Jesus whom you murdered by hanging on a tree. Him God has exalted to His right hand to be Prince and Savior, to give repentance to Israel and forgiveness of sins. And we are His witnesses to these things, and so also is the Holy Spirit whom God has given to those who obey Him."

When the Jewish leaders heard this, they were furious and plotted to kill the apostles. Then a teacher of the law named Gamaliel, a man respected by all the people, stood up in the council and commanded that the apostles be put outside for a while. Then he said, "Men of Israel, take heed to yourselves what you intend to do regarding these men. . . . I say to you, keep away from these men and let them alone; for if this plan or this work is of men, it will come to nothing; but if it is of God, you cannot overthrow it— lest you even be found to fight against God."

The members of the council agreed with these convincing words. They decided to be cautious in their punishment. Therefore, they had the apostles brought in and whipped. Then they commanded Peter and the other apostles not to speak again in the name of Jesus.

But the Jewish leaders could not stop the followers of Jesus Christ. The apostles went out from the council rejoicing that they could suffer in the name of Jesus. They did not miss a single day of teaching and preaching in the temple, telling everyone the good news about the Savior of the world.

As the months went by, the number of church members grew. Problems came up that had to be faced. The poor and the needy had to be cared for, and the widows and orphans required food and clothing. Because the apostles had to give so much attention to this work, they did not have much time to tell the story of Jesus. At last they said, "It is not desirable that we should leave the word of God and serve tables. Therefore, brethren, seek out from among you seven men of good reputation, full of the Holy Spirit and wisdom, whom we may appoint over this business." The plan was approved, and seven good men of the church were selected to take care of the poor and the needy.

Among the seven was Stephen, a man of great faith and power, who did miracles among the people. The Jewish leaders of a synagogue called the Synagogue of the Freedmen tried to argue with Stephen about Jesus. But they could not answer the wisdom and Spirit by which Stephen spoke. Secretly they convinced some men to spread a rumor that Stephen had spoken blasphemous words. After stirring up the scribes and teachers of the law against him, they had Stephen arrested and brought before the council. False witnesses came forward and accused him, saying, "This man does not cease to speak blasphemous words against this holy place and the law."

GOD SAYS:

" ' "Be faithful until death, and I will give you the crown of life." ' "
–Revelation 2:10

Everyone on the council stared at Stephen. His face looked like the face of an angel. The high priest found his voice and asked, "Are these things so?"

"Brethren and fathers, listen," said Stephen. "The God of glory appeared to our father Abraham when he was in Mesopotamia, before he dwelt in Haran, and said to him, 'Get out of your country and from your relatives, and come to a land that I will show you.' Then he came out of the land of the Chaldeans and dwelt in Haran. And from there, when his father was dead, He moved him to this land in which you now dwell." Then Stephen went on to recount the history of the Jewish people from Abraham down to the time of Solomon and the building of the temple. Finally Stephen said, "You stiff-necked and uncircumcised in heart and ears! You always resist the Holy Spirit; as your fathers did, so do you. Which of the prophets did your fathers not persecute? And they killed those who foretold the coming of the Just One, of whom you now have become the betrayers and murderers, who have received the law by the direction of angels and have not kept it."

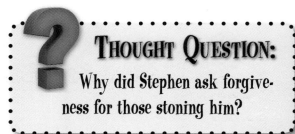

THOUGHT QUESTION: Why did Stephen ask forgiveness for those stoning him?

The leaders were furious and ground their teeth at Stephen. But he, being full of the Holy Spirit, gazed up and could see into heaven. He saw with his own eyes the glory of God and Jesus standing by God's right hand. "Look!" he said excitedly, "I see the heavens opened and the Son of Man standing at the right hand of God!"

The council members began to shout and put their fingers in their ears. Then all of them rushed at Stephen. They dragged him out of the city to the pit where criminals were stoned. Throwing the disciple into the pit, they picked up stones and hurled them at Stephen. The men who were there laid their coats down on the ground at the feet of a young man named Saul of Tarsus.

As the stones crushed Stephen's body, he fell on his knees and prayed, "Lord, do not charge them with this sin." After he said this, he died.

PHILIP MEETS A QUEEN'S TREASURER

Acts 8

Saul of Tarsus not only agreed with the stoning of Stephen. He also led the fight against other followers of Jesus. He went from house to house arresting the church members and dragging them off to prison.

The persecution in Jerusalem became severe. It prompted most of the apostles and church members to move out of the city. In other towns and villages they could tell the story of the Mighty Prince without being arrested.

Among the seven men chosen to care for the poor and needy in the church was Philip the evangelist. He was among those who left Jerusalem, and he went to the city of Samaria to preach about Jesus. Crowds of people listened to him and accepted his message. Through the power of the Holy Spirit, Philip healed the sick and made the lame walk.

There was a magician in Samaria, whose sorcery had amazed the people for a long time. When this man heard the story of Jesus, he believed it and was baptized into the

NORMAN BRICE

church. He hung around with Philip, watching with awe the miracles the preacher performed.

The apostles who were still in Jerusalem heard how people in Samaria had accepted the word of God. They sent Peter and John to visit the new church members and pray for them to receive the Holy Spirit. When Simon saw how the Holy Spirit came upon the people when the apostles prayed, he offered Peter some money. He said, "Give me this power also, that anyone on whom I lay hands may receive the Holy Spirit."

"Your money perish with you," said Peter sharply, "because you thought that the gift of God could be purchased with money! You have neither part nor portion in this matter, for your heart is not right in the sight of God. Repent therefore of this your wickedness, and pray God if perhaps the thought of your heart may be forgiven you."

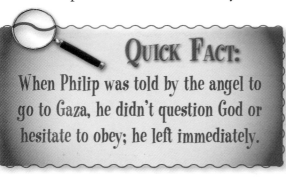

QUICK FACT:
When Philip was told by the angel to go to Gaza, he didn't question God or hesitate to obey; he left immediately.

Simon, who did not understand God's gift, was sorry for his mistake. "Pray to the Lord for me," he begged, "that none of the things which you have spoken may come upon me." The word *simony* means trying to buy a position in the church, and it came from this experience.

One day while Philip was in Samaria, an angel told him to go south on the desert road that runs from Jerusalem to Gaza. Philip obeyed at once, although he did not know where he was going or why he was making the trip.

Candace, the queen of Ethiopia, had sent her chief treasurer to Jerusalem to worship at the temple. He was then returning to Ethiopia, a country to the south of Egypt. As he rode in his chariot, the treasurer was reading a scroll of the prophecies of Isaiah. Philip

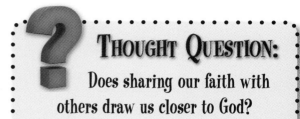

THOUGHT QUESTION: Does sharing our faith with others draw us closer to God?

saw the official riding by, and the Holy Spirit said to him, "Go near and overtake this chariot."

Philip ran to the chariot and heard the Ethiopian reading the scroll out loud. "Do you understand what you are reading?" he called out.

"How can I, unless someone guides me?" the official responded. He invited Philip to get into the chariot and sit with him. The preacher saw that the scroll was opened to these words of the Old Testament prophet:

> "He was led as a lamb to the slaughter;
> And as a sheep before its shearer is silent,
> So He opened not His mouth."

The treasurer asked, "Of whom does the prophet say this, of himself or of some other man?"

Philip explained that it was a prophecy about Jesus. He told the story of how the Messiah came to earth and died to take away the sin of the world.

The chariot rolled along near an oasis in the desert. The Ethiopian said, "See, here is water. What hinders me from being baptized?"

"If you believe with all your heart, you may," Philip replied.

The officer ordered the chariot to be stopped. Then he and Philip went into the water, and Philip baptized this new follower of Jesus. After they came up out of the water, Philip was taken away immediately by the Spirit. The eunuch didn't see him anymore. Commanding that his chariot move on, the official went on his way rejoicing.

Philip appeared at Azotus, a town north of Gaza, and preached in all the towns nearby, until he came to Caesarea.

A New Apostle for Christ

Acts 9:1–31; 22:1–21

Messengers of the high priest traveled quickly along the road from Jerusalem to Damascus. They were led by Saul, the young man from Tarsus. Full of energy and determination, Saul pushed forward as fast as he could. He was anxious to reach Damascus in Syria because of the letters he was carrying. They were letters from the high priest to the leaders of the Damascus synagogue, giving Saul the power to arrest the followers of Jesus. He could bind them in chains and return them to Jerusalem for trial.

This fiery young leader had been educated in the Jewish law by Gamaliel. Saul believed that he was doing the work of God by putting the believers in prison. He would stamp out the new movement before it spread very far.

About noon, as the travelers came near Damascus, a brilliant flash of light came down from heaven. Saul fell to the ground, and then he heard a Voice saying to him, "Saul, Saul, why are you persecuting Me?"

"Who are You, Lord?" Saul asked.

"I am Jesus, whom you are persecuting," said the Voice.

Trembling with fear, Saul asked, "Lord, what do You want me to do?"

"Arise and go into the city, and you will be told what you must do."

The men traveling with Saul stood speechless. They had heard the Voice but saw no one. Saul got up off the ground and realized that he could not see anything. In that flash of glorious light, the man of Tarsus had met the Son of God face to face, and his eyes could not bear it.

Saul's companions took him by the hand and led him into the city. They went to a house on Straight Street. There Saul stayed for three days, without his sight, neither eating nor drinking during that time.

On the third day, blind Saul was lying on his bed in his room. There was a knock on the front door, and a man asked for him. It was Ananias, a faithful disciple of Jesus, who had been told in a vision to go and help Saul.

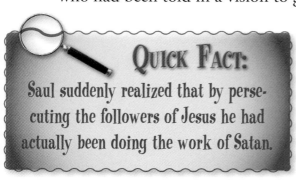

QUICK FACT:
Saul suddenly realized that by persecuting the followers of Jesus he had actually been doing the work of Satan.

At first Ananias was afraid to visit the blind man. He knew that Saul had come to Damascus to arrest the followers of Jesus. Certainly his own name was on the list of those who were to go to prison. But with assurance from God, he obeyed and came to help the persecutor.

Placing his hands on Saul, Ananias said, "Brother Saul, the Lord Jesus, who appeared to you on the road as you came, has sent me that you may

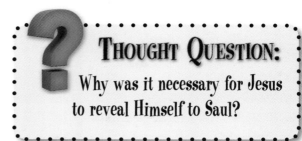

THOUGHT QUESTION:
Why was it necessary for Jesus to reveal Himself to Saul?

receive your sight and be filled with the Holy Spirit."

Something like scales dropped away from Saul's eyes, and he could see again. He got up from his bed and was baptized that very day.

Saul's plans were now completely changed. Instead of hating Jesus and persecuting His followers, Saul went into the synagogue at Damascus and preached the story of the Savior. He was able to prove from the writings of the ancient prophets that Jesus was the true Messiah.

Naturally, the believers were afraid of Saul. They said, "Is this not he who destroyed those who called on this name in Jerusalem, and has come here for that purpose, so that he might bring them bound to the chief priests?"

Saul stayed with church members for some time. His preaching confounded the Damascus Jews who were allied with the high priest in Jerusalem. They had no argument against his message. Thinking they could be rid of the new disciple, they plotted to kill him. They watched the gates of the city day and night to catch him.

Saul found out about the plot, and he decided to leave for Jerusalem. Late one night, the Damascus disciples took him to the city wall and let him down to the outside in a large basket.

When Saul arrived in Jerusalem, he tried to join the disciples there. But they were afraid of him and did not believe he was a disciple of Jesus. Finally, Barnabas took Saul to the apostles and vouched for him, describing how the young man had seen the Lord on the road and had preached the story of Jesus in Damascus. So, he was accepted

by the church in Jerusalem and preached often there.

Some Hellenists who were opposed to the message of Jesus plotted to kill Saul. When church members discovered the plot, they helped him escape from the city. He went to Caesarea and then on to his hometown of Tarsus.

The churches in Judea, Galilee, and Samaria went through a time of peace. Filled with reverence for God, and aided by the Holy Spirit, the apostles preached the good news about Jesus, and the churches grew with new converts.

PETER, CHAMPION OF TRUTH

Acts 9:32–12:19

The apostle Peter traveled around the country, visiting the followers of Christ who had been forced to leave Jerusalem. At the small town of Lydda, Peter met a man named Aeneas, who had been paralyzed and bedridden for eight years. Standing at the bedside of the man, he said, "Aeneas, Jesus the Christ heals you. Arise and make your bed."

Strength surged into the weak body, and immediately Aeneas got up from his bed. Soon everyone in the village and the people in the surrounding country came to see the man who had been healed. Because of this miracle they listened to Peter's story of Jesus, and many accepted it.

One day, two men came to Peter from the nearby town of Joppa. This was the thriving seaport to which, centuries earlier, King Hiram had sent rafts of cedar logs for Solomon's temple. The two visitors told Peter about a woman in Joppa named Tabitha, whose name in Greek is translated Dorcas. She had spent her life making clothes for the poor and helping the sick and the needy. But she had become sick and died, and her body was awaiting burial. The men begged Peter to go back with them, and he agreed.

When they arrived at Tabitha's house, they found the widows and the poor people weeping over the death of their dear friend. The people showed Peter the coats and clothes Tabitha had made. Then the apostle sent all the people from the room, and he knelt and prayed to God. Turning to the body of the dead woman, he said, "Tabitha, arise."

Immediately she opened her eyes; and when she saw Peter, she sat up. The apostle took her by the hand and helped her to her feet. When he called in all the believers waiting outside, he presented the woman to them alive and well.

Soon all the people of Joppa heard about Tabitha, and they were ready to listen to Peter's message. The apostle decided to stay in the seaport for some time, and he lodged with a man named Simon, who was a tanner.

While Peter was at Simon's house in Joppa, something strange was taking place over in the city of Caesarea. A captain of the Roman army named Cornelius lived in that city, and he loved and obeyed God.

QUICK FACT: Although Cornelius was a wealthy captain in the Roman army, he had given his heart to God and was known for his generosity to the poor.

One afternoon about three o'clock, while he was praying, he had a vision and saw an angel, who said to him, "Cornelius!"

"What is it, lord?" the captain asked, feeling afraid.

"Your prayers and your alms have come up for a memorial before God," the angel answered. "Now send men to Joppa, and send for Simon whose surname is Peter. He is lodging with

JOE MANISCALCO

Simon, a tanner, whose house is by the sea. He will tell you what you must do."

When the angel had gone, Cornelius called two of his servants and a soldier of his bodyguard. He explained to them what the angel had said and sent them to Joppa to find Peter.

The next day about noon, while the three men were traveling toward Joppa, Peter climbed the steps to the top of Simon's house to pray. He was very hungry and wanted to eat. While he was waiting for food to be prepared, he received a vision. He saw the heavens opened and a large sheet lowered to the ground by the four corners. In the sheet were all kinds of animals, reptiles, and wild birds. A Voice spoke to Peter, saying, "Rise, Peter; kill and eat."

"Not so, Lord!" said Peter. "For I have never eaten anything common or unclean." By this, Peter meant that he had always eaten foods that were clean according to the Law of Moses.

The Voice came to him again. "What God has cleansed you must not call common."

The strange vision was repeated three times, and then the sheet was taken back up to heaven.

While Peter sat wondering what the vision meant, the servants of Captain Cornelius arrived at Simon's house. They asked to see the man named Simon Peter. At that moment, the Holy Spirit said to Peter that three men were looking for him, and he should go down, meet them, and go with them.

Peter went downstairs and met the three men. He said,

"Yes, I am he whom you seek. For what reason have you come?"

One of them answered, "Cornelius the centurion, a just man, one who fears God and has a good reputation among all the nation of the Jews, was divinely instructed by a holy angel to summon you to his house, and to hear words from you."

Peter invited the men in to stay the night, and the next day they started back to Caesarea. The apostle took six church members from Joppa along with him. When they arrived, Cornelius was waiting for them. He welcomed Peter and fell at his feet to worship him. But Peter lifted him up and said, "Stand up; I myself am also a man."

Then Cornelius brought him into the house. The captain had invited his relatives and close friends to his home to hear

GOD SAYS:

" 'God shows no partiality. But in every nation whoever fears Him and works righteousness is accepted by Him.' " –Acts 10:34, 35

what Peter might say. He described to the apostle the visit by a "man in bright clothing" who instructed him to find Peter and invite him to his house. "So I sent to you immediately," Cornelius said, "and you have done well to come. Now therefore, we are all present before God, to hear all the things commanded you by God."

Peter was amazed at what the captain had said. "In truth I perceive," said Peter, "that God shows no partiality. But in every nation whoever fears Him and works righteousness is accepted by Him." Now the apostle understood his vision of the animals to mean that no one of any nation or race was "unclean." All are loved by God.

He told the family of Cornelius about Jesus of Nazareth and how God had anointed Him with the Holy Spirit and with power. "He went about doing good and healing all who were oppressed by the devil, for God was with Him," said Peter. "And we are witnesses of all things which He did both in the land of the Jews and in Jerusalem, whom they killed by hanging on a tree. Him God raised up on the third day, and showed Him openly, not to all the people, but to witnesses chosen before by God, even to us who ate and drank with Him after He arose from the dead." Through Jesus, Peter explained, all who believe in His name will receive forgiveness of their sins.

While Peter was still speaking, the Holy Spirit came upon everyone in the room. The Jewish believers from Joppa were astonished to see this wonderful gift poured out on Gentiles, or non-Jewish people.

After the meeting, Cornelius and his family were baptized, and Peter stayed with them for several days more.

The church members and apostles back in Judea heard that some non-Jews had become believers and received the Holy Spirit. When Peter returned to Jerusalem, Jews who followed the laws very strictly came to argue with him. "You went in to uncircumcised men and ate with them!" they sputtered.

The apostle described his experience from beginning to end—about the vision he received, the angel who visited Cornelius, and the meeting he had with the captain's family

and friends. Peter explained that he was certain God had given His message of love to every person no matter what their race or nationality. He ended by saying, "If therefore God gave them the same gift as He gave us when we believed on the Lord Jesus Christ, who was I that I could withstand God?" When the Jews of Jerusalem heard this, they became silent. The church members, however, praised God and said, "Then God has also granted to the Gentiles repentance to life."

About this time King Herod began to persecute the church. He arrested the apostle James, brother of John, and put him to death. Then, seeing that this

pleased the Jewish leaders, the king decided to arrest Peter also. During Passover that year, while Peter was in Jerusalem, Roman soldiers seized him and put him in jail. Four squads of soldiers were put on guard. Herod planned to bring the apostle before the crowds after the Passover Feast and put him to death.

THOUGHT QUESTION:

Why did Peter show himself to the church members in Jerusalem first before fleeing the city?

While Peter was in prison, the church members prayed constantly that God would save his life. On the night before Herod was to bring him before the people, Peter was asleep between two soldiers, fastened to them with two chains. Other soldiers stood in front of the door. Suddenly an angel of God stood by the apostle, and a light shone in the dungeon. The angel tapped Peter on his side, pulled him upright, saying, "Arise quickly!"

The chains dropped from Peter's hands, and the angel said, "Put on your belt and your sandals!" Dazed by the sudden awakening, Peter did as he was told. Then the angel said, "Put on your garment and follow me."

Peter followed the angel without realizing what was taking place. He thought he was having a dream. They passed the first guard and then the second guard and came to the iron gate that led out to the street. The iron gate swung open by itself, and the angel and Peter walked out together. They went down the street, and then suddenly the angel was gone. Peter came to himself and thought, "Now I know for certain that the Lord has sent His angel, and has delivered me from the hand of Herod and from all the expectation of the Jewish people."

Peter hurried through the dark streets to the home of Mary, the mother of John Mark, a young leader in the church. Many church members had gathered there to pray. When Peter knocked at the door, a girl named Rhoda came to answer. When she recognized Peter's voice, she was so happy that she did not open the door. Instead, she ran back and told the group that Peter was standing outside.

They told her she was crazy, but she kept insisting that it was true. So they said, "It is his angel!"

All this time Peter kept knocking at the door. When they opened it, the believers were astonished. Peter motioned to them to keep silent, and he came in and told them how God had brought him out of prison. Then he said Goodbye to them and went to another house. Before dawn, Peter had left the city to escape recapture by King Herod's soldiers, and he set out for Caesarea.

As soon as it was daylight, a great stir went through Jerusalem. The guards could not explain what had happened to their prisoner. Herod ordered a thorough search for Peter, but he could not be found. The king was so angry that he ordered the guards of the jail to be put to death.

UNDER MARCHING ORDERS

Acts 11:19–30; 13

Saul had been accepted as a preacher by the church in Jerusalem. While he was still there, he spoke fearlessly about Jesus to the Greek-educated Jews. These men hated the apostle's message, and they planned to kill him.

Saul did not want to be silent. However, one day as he was praying in the temple court, he fell into a trance. He saw the Lord saying to him, "Make haste and get out of Jerusalem quickly, for they will not receive your testimony concerning Me."

"Lord, they know that in every synagogue I imprisoned and beat those who believe on You," Saul responded. "And when the blood of Your martyr Stephen was shed, I also was standing by consenting to his death, and guarding the clothes of those who were killing him."

But the answer came from God, "Depart, for I will send you far from here to the Gentiles." This was the time Saul escaped the city in a basket. He left on the long trip northward to Caesarea and on to Tarsus, his hometown. There he stayed for many months.

Some of the church members who had scattered from Jerusalem traveled into Syria. They went as far as the busy city of Antioch, about a hundred sixty miles north of Damascus. Antioch was a beautiful city, the third largest in the Roman Empire. It was surrounded by a wall many miles long, and its streets were paved with white marble. The city was famous for magnificent temples, rich palaces, and lush gardens. The followers of Jesus began to preach in that great city. As they told the

story of the Master's life and death, a large number of people believed.

Soon the news of what was happening in Antioch reached Jerusalem. The apostles who were still there decided to send Barnabas to visit the believers in Antioch. When he arrived and saw the many new believers, he gave thanks to God. Barnabas went on to Tarsus, found Saul, and brought him back to Antioch. For a year the two men taught the people, and a strong church was established. It was in Antioch that the believers were first called Christians.

> **GOD SAYS:**
> " ' "I will also give You as a light to the Gentiles, that You should be My salvation to the ends of the earth." ' "
> —Isaiah 49:6

About this time a great famine spread throughout the Roman Empire. The land of Palestine was severely affected by the lack of rain and the crop failures. Many of the poor church members in Jerusalem and the surrounding towns suffered from hunger. The disciples in Antioch collected gifts to send as relief to the church members in Judea. Saul and Barnabas carried the gifts to the church elders in Jerusalem. For some time the two men stayed in the city to help those in need. When their work was finished, they returned to Antioch, taking young John Mark, a cousin of Barnabas, with them.

Several prophets and teachers were working in the church at Antioch, including Saul and Barnabas. One day as the teachers were praying together, the Holy Spirit said,

"Now separate to Me Barnabas and Saul for the work to which I have called them." After fasting and praying, the teachers laid their hands on the heads of the two men. This meant that they were dedicating them to a special work. Since Saul was going to preach among the Greek-speaking people, he took the Greek form of his name. From then on he was called Paul.

Prompted by the Holy Spirit, the two missionaries left Antioch, taking John Mark with them. They went to Seleucia, a town on the coast of the Mediterranean Sea. There they took passage on a boat sailing to the island of Cyprus, the home of Barnabas. Paul, Barnabas, and John Mark traveled through the whole island.

When they came to Paphos, the capital city, they met a Jewish magician named Elymas, a close friend of the Roman governor. Now the governor, Sergius Paulus, said he wanted to hear about Jesus. But Elymas tried to get in the way and keep him from hearing God's message.

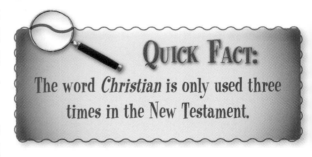

QUICK FACT:
The word *Christian* is only used three times in the New Testament.

Paul, filled with the Holy Spirit, looked intently at Elymas and said, "O full of all deceit and all fraud, you son of the devil, you enemy of all righteousness, will you not cease perverting the straight ways of the Lord? And now, indeed, the hand of the Lord is upon you, and you shall be blind, not seeing the sun for a time."

Instantly a dark mist fell on Elymas. He groped about for someone to lead him by the hand. The governor was astounded by what had happened, and he believed the good news of Jesus.

Paul, Barnabas, and John Mark took a boat out of Paphos and sailed north to Asia Minor. They visited Perga, a town on the Cestrus River. It was here that young John Mark said Goodbye to his companions and returned to Jerusalem. Paul and Barnabas pushed on to another place named Antioch, a small town in the region of Pisidia.

THOUGHT QUESTION:

Why were the Jews in Antioch so jealous of Paul and Barnabas?

On the Sabbath day the two apostles went to the synagogue in Antioch and sat down. After a reading from the Law and the Prophets, the synagogue rulers said to Paul and Barnabas, "Men and brethren, if you have any word of exhortation for the people, say on."

Paul stood up and began to speak. He reviewed the history of Israel from the time of the Exodus down to the appearance of Jesus. He spoke about the hope of the Messiah. Then he said, "Men and brethren, sons of the family of Abraham, and those among you who fear God, to you the word of this salvation has been sent."

In this first recorded speech of Paul, he related how Jesus had been crucified and had risen from the tomb. Finally he said to them, "We declare to you glad tidings—that promise which was made to the fathers. God has fulfilled this for us their children, in that He has raised up Jesus."

When the meeting was over, the people came up to Paul and Barnabas. They begged them to speak more about Jesus the next Sabbath. That week the two missionaries talked with many of the Jews and devout Gentiles and urged them to continue in the grace of God.

The next Sabbath nearly the whole town gathered to hear God's message. This made the synagogue leaders jealous, and they spoke strongly against what Paul was saying. But Paul and Barnabas answered them boldly. "It was necessary that the word of God should be spoken to you first; but since you reject it, and judge yourselves unworthy of

everlasting life, behold, we turn to the Gentiles. For so the Lord has commanded us:

> 'I have set you as a light to the Gentiles,
> That you should be for salvation to the ends of
>   the earth.' "

When the people of Antioch—those who were not Jews—heard Paul say this, they were very happy. They thanked God that the promise of eternal life had been given to them too.

The message of the Lord spread around that region. However, the jealous Jews stirred up opposition among the leaders of Antioch. Finally, they convinced the leading men to expel Paul and Barnabas from the town. Shaking the dust off their feet as they left, Paul and Barnabas set out for the city of Iconium. The disciples there welcomed them with great happiness.

HATED AND STONED

Acts 14

Paul and Barnabas were now traveling in a country where some mean, rough people lived. Towns were scattered far apart. Travelers were in danger of attacks by bandits on the long, lonely roads.

At Iconium the two missionaries were welcomed as they had been at first in Antioch of Pisidia. But after a time, the Jews who refused to accept the story of Jesus stirred up hatred against the apostles. Soon the town was divided between those who were for Paul and Barnabas and those who were against them. One day a noisy mob, shouting insults and threatening to stone the Christians, gathered where the town's officials could see them. They hoped to cause so much trouble that the officials would force Paul and Barnabas to leave. The apostles were urged by their friends to go, so they slipped out of town. Making their way across the mountains, they came to the cities of Lystra and Derbe.

At Lystra, the Greek inhabitants mistakenly thought the apostles were preaching about their heathen gods. As

Paul was speaking, he saw a man sitting nearby who could neither stand nor walk. The apostle, looking at the man intently, saw that he had great faith to be healed.

"Stand up straight on your feet!" Paul commanded in a loud voice.

Immediately the man jumped up and began to walk around. The crowd, seeing what had happened, and thinking of their Greek gods, shouted, "The gods have come down to us in the likeness of men!" According to the Greek religion, the gods sometimes came down and visited the earth.

GOD SAYS:

" 'Blessed are you when they revile and persecute you, and say all kinds of evil against you falsely for My sake.' " -Matthew 5:11

The people of Lystra declared that Barnabas was Zeus, and that Paul was Hermes, because he was the chief speaker. Soon the priest of Zeus, eager to show gratitude, came from the pagan temple leading sacred bulls, while boys and girls followed carrying garlands of flowers. They intended to offer sacrifices to the two men.

When Paul and Barnabas saw the crowd and realized what was happening, they rushed in among the multitude. Tearing their clothes, they shouted, "Men, why are you doing these things? We also are men with the same nature as you, and preach to you that you should turn from these useless things to the living God, who made the heaven, the earth, the sea, and all things that are in them, who in bygone generations allowed all nations to walk in their own

ways. Nevertheless He did not leave Himself without witness, in that He did good, gave us rain from heaven and fruitful seasons, filling our hearts with food and gladness."

Even these words of Paul could scarcely keep the crowd from worshiping the apostles. The good feelings did not last long, however. Some Jews from Antioch in Pisidia and Iconium came to town and stirred up hatred among the people. Those who, only a little while before, had planned to offer sacrifices to Paul and Barnabas now picked up stones and began to throw them at Paul. Some of the rocks struck him, and he fell on the pavement unconscious. Thinking he was dead, the mob dragged him outside the city wall. The Christian believers gathered around him, and Paul got up and walked back into the town.

A young man of Lystra had heard the story of Jesus and accepted it. He knew how the apostles had been treated at Antioch and Iconium, but he was not afraid to join them. He stood by the unconscious Paul after the mob had dragged the apostle out of the town. This youth, named Timothy, decided to be a soldier of the cross.

From childhood, Timothy had been taught the Law and the Prophets by his mother and his grandmother. After hearing Paul speak, he believed that Jesus was the Messiah, the Lamb of God who would save the world.

The next day Paul and Barnabas hiked on to Derbe, where they told the good news of Jesus, and a number of the people believed. Then the missionaries turned back and revisited Lystra, Iconium, and Antioch in Pisidia. It took courage to do this, because their enemies were waiting for them in each of these towns. But they went ahead, visiting and encouraging the Christian believers and appointing

QUICK FACT:
The Jews' efforts to stop the work of Paul and Barnabas only caused more people to believe.

leaders in each church. They urged members to endure hardships for Jesus Christ, saying, "We must through many tribulations en- ter the kingdom of God."

The two men re- traced their path through Pisidia and Pamphylia, finally sail-

THOUGHT QUESTION:
How do hardships help us "enter the kingdom of heaven"?

ing back to the big city of Antioch in Syria, where they had started their journey. Paul and Barnabas gathered the disciples in the church there and reported their journey. They described what they had accomplished in the cities through the Holy Spirit. God had opened "the way of faith" for the Gentiles, the non-Jews, everywhere.

Seventeen years had passed since Paul was blinded on the road to Damascus by the glory of Jesus. The apostle seems to have had some illness that he never overcame. In spite of this, he traveled far around the known world of his time, enduring suffering and hardship, punishment and imprisonment, in order to tell the story of his Savior. Paul, the fearless soldier of the cross, once said to the church members, "I determined not to know anything among you except Jesus Christ and Him crucified" (1 Corinthians 2:2).

TURNING THE WORLD UPSIDE DOWN

Acts 15:35–17:15

After spending some time in Jerusalem at a council of the church leaders, Paul and Barnabas returned to Antioch to help the disciples there. One day Paul said to Barnabas, "Let us now go back and visit our brethren in every city where we have preached the word of the Lord, and see how they are doing."

Barnabas agreed, and he suggested that they take John Mark with them. But Paul refused to allow the young man to go along. He was unhappy that John Mark had deserted them at Perga on the previous trip and gone home. So, after an argument, the two apostles parted ways. Paul took Silas with him, while Barnabas sailed to Cyprus with his young cousin John Mark. Paul and Silas traveled through the land of Syria and finally reached Lystra and Derbe.

At Lystra the missionaries again met young Timothy, who was still true to the faith. The young disciple was well spoken of by the church members there. Paul liked the young man and called him his "own son in the faith." He wanted Timothy to travel with him and Silas. The three men visited all the churches in that region, encouraging the Christians.

The missionaries reached the town of Troas, a port on the Aegean Sea. There they could look across the blue waters toward the mainland of Greece. That night Paul had a vision. He seemed to see a man from the distant land of Macedonia.

The figure was holding out his hands and pleading, "Come over to Macedonia and help us."

In a few days Paul, Silas, Timothy, and Doctor Luke, who had now joined them, sailed from Troas. Doctor Luke was the writer of the Gospel of Luke and the book of Acts in the Bible. After stopping at ports along the way, the four men landed at Philippi, the biggest city in that part of Macedonia. It was an important outpost of the Roman Empire, with a garrison of soldiers stationed there.

On the Sabbath the missionaries went down to the river and spoke to some women who often met there to pray. A woman named Lydia had come from the nearby town of Thyatira to hear Paul's story of Jesus. She was in the business of selling purple dyes. Upon hearing Paul's message, she believed, and soon she and her family were baptized. Afterward she convinced the missionaries to come and stay at her house for a while.

One day, as the missionaries were walking down the street in Thyatira, they met a slave girl who was possessed by an evil spirit. Her fortune-telling made her masters a great amount of money. The girl followed Paul and his friends, crying out, "These men are the servants of the Most High God, who proclaim to us the way of salvation." She followed them around the city for several days, repeating this phrase over and over.

GOD SAYS:
"Let no one despise your youth, but be an example to the believers in word, in conduct, in love, in spirit, in faith, in purity." –1 Timothy 4:12

Paul and Silas were out walking on another day, and Paul became greatly annoyed by the evil spirit. He turned and said to the spirit, "I command you in the name of Jesus Christ to come out of her." And the evil spirit left her.

When her masters saw that they could no longer make profit by the girl's psychic powers, they seized Paul and Silas and dragged them into the central marketplace. Presenting the two men to the magistrates of the town, they said, "These men, being Jews, exceedingly trouble our city; and they teach customs which are not lawful for us, being Romans, to receive or observe."

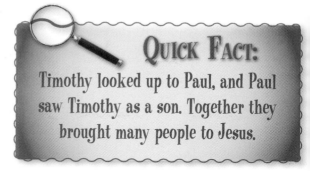

QUICK FACT:
Timothy looked up to Paul, and Paul saw Timothy as a son. Together they brought many people to Jesus.

People began to gather 'round, and soon the crowd turned mean. So, without holding a legal hearing, the officials had Paul and Silas stripped of their shirts and beaten with rods. After a severe beating, the two missionaries were thrown into prison. The jailer received orders to keep close watch over them. He hustled them into the inner jail cell and fastened their feet in stocks.

During the night, although they were suffering great pain from bleeding wounds, Paul and Silas sang hymns and prayed. They were still awake at midnight when a great earthquake shook the jail to its foundations. All of the doors flew open, and the chains of every prisoner came loose. The jailer woke up, and he saw the doors of the jail wide open. Assuming that all the prisoners had escaped, in complete despair he grabbed his sword to kill himself.

Paul shouted to the jailer, "Do yourself no harm, for we are all here." None of the prisoners had moved.

The jailer put his sword down and called for a light. Then he ran into the jail and bowed trembling before Paul and Silas. He led them outside and said, "Sirs, what must I do to be saved?"

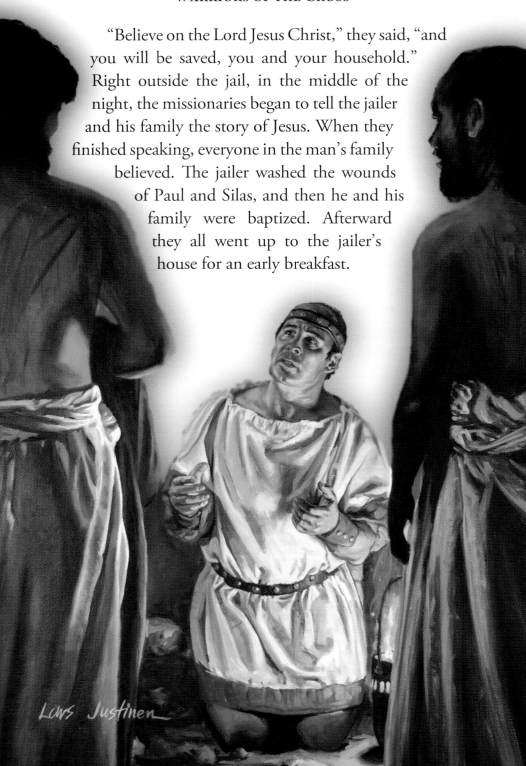

"Believe on the Lord Jesus Christ," they said, "and you will be saved, you and your household." Right outside the jail, in the middle of the night, the missionaries began to tell the jailer and his family the story of Jesus. When they finished speaking, everyone in the man's family believed. The jailer washed the wounds of Paul and Silas, and then he and his family were baptized. Afterward they all went up to the jailer's house for an early breakfast.

Lars Justinen

In the morning, officers from the town came to Paul and said, "The magistrates have sent to let you go. Now therefore depart, and go in peace."

The apostle, however, refused to be treated this way. He said, "They have beaten us openly, uncondemned Romans, and have thrown us into prison. And now do they put us out secretly? No indeed! Let them come themselves and get us out."

The officers delivered Paul's message to the city magistrates. They became afraid when they heard that Paul and Silas were Roman citizens. The magistrates hurried to the jail and begged the apostles to leave town at once. But the missionaries would not be hurried away like that. They went first to Lydia's house and gathered the church members together and encouraged them. Afterward they set out toward the city of Thessalonica.

For three Sabbaths they preached the good news in the synagogue of Thessalonica. Using the Scriptures, they taught about Jesus, the Messiah, and how He suffered, died, and rose from the dead. "This Jesus whom I preach to you," said Paul, "is the Christ." Some of the people in Thessalonica believed, and they joined Paul and Silas. Special interest in the message rose up among the Greeks who believed in God. Some of the leading women believed in Jesus, as well.

But as in other towns, the Jews who did not believe the message grew envious and stirred up trouble. They found some of the most evil men in Thessalonica and incited them to start a riot. Soon the whole city was in an uproar. An angry mob attacked the house of Jason, one of the

Christian disciples, and searched it, hoping to find Paul and Silas. When they did not find the missionaries, they dragged Jason and some other church members to the town leaders. They shouted, "These who have turned the world upside down have come here too. Jason has harbored them, and these are all acting contrary to the decrees of Caesar, saying there is another king—Jesus."

The crowd roared at these words. Hoping to be rid of the trouble, the officials forced Jason and the other Christians to pay bond money and then released them. That night the church members sent Paul and Silas away to Berea, another city not far away.

THOUGHT QUESTION:

Why did Paul and the other prisoners stay in prison when they could have escaped?

At Berea the apostles went to the Jewish synagogue. The Jews of that city were more fair-minded than those at Thessalonica. They listened to the message and studied the Scriptures to find out if Paul's preaching was correct. Many of the Jews, as well as some of the Greek men and women, believed Jesus to be the Messiah. But it was not long before nonbelieving Jews in Thessalonica heard about the preaching in Berea. They came and stirred up crowds of people as they had done before. Once more Paul had to hurry away, this time to the seacoast. Silas and Timothy stayed behind to finish their work. Some of the church members went with Paul to Athens, where the apostle waited for Silas and Timothy to join him.

PAUL, PREACHER AND TENTMAKER

Acts 17:16–18:21

The city of Athens was once the center of art and culture in the ancient world. In Paul's time much of its glory had gone away. The Romans had destroyed much of the beauty and grandeur of this capital city when they conquered it. However, the people of Athens still loved art, poetry, and philosophy.

As the apostle Paul wandered around the streets of Athens, he saw statues of pagan gods and magnificent temples and altars. War victories and heroic deeds were memorialized by sculptures and shrines. The apostle of Jesus Christ was distressed to see a city full of idols.

On Sabbaths he discussed the Scriptures with Jews and God-fearing Greeks. On weekdays Paul went to the public square and debated with whoever happened to be there. To those who would listen, Paul told the story of Jesus and how He died and rose from the dead.

Some of the Greek philosophers who heard him said, "What does this babbler want to say?" By this they meant that Paul had spoken ideas that were strange and new to them.

"He seems to be a proclaimer of foreign gods," others said.

Finally, some of the men of Athens took Paul to the council of Areopagus on Mars' Hill. This was an important place for Athenians and foreigners alike to discuss new ideas. "May we know what this new doctrine is of which you

speak?" the men asked. "For you are bringing some strange things to our ears. Therefore we want to know what these things mean."

Paul stood up in the council and began to speak in a polite, careful manner. He said, "Men of Athens, I perceive that in all things you are very religious;

GOD SAYS:

" 'Therefore, the One whom you worship without knowing, Him I proclaim to you.' " –Acts 17:23

for as I was passing through and considering the objects of your worship, I even found an altar with this inscription: TO THE UNKNOWN GOD. Therefore, the One whom you worship without knowing, Him I proclaim to you."

The apostle continued to explain. "God, who made the world and everything in it," he said, "since He is Lord of heaven and earth, does not dwell in temples made with hands. Nor is He worshiped with men's hands, as though He needed anything, since He gives to all life, breath, and all things."

The men of Athens listened carefully. Paul quoted from some of the Greek poets, and finally he spoke against the worship of idols. "Since we are the offspring of God," he said, "we ought not to think that the Divine Nature is like gold or silver or stone, something shaped by art and man's devising. Truly, these times of ignorance God overlooked, but now commands all men everywhere to repent, because He has appointed a day on which He will judge the world in righteousness by the Man whom He has ordained. He has given assurance of this to all by raising Him from the dead."

As soon as Paul mentioned Jesus being raised from the

dead, some of the people mocked him. But others said, "We will hear you again on this matter."

Paul left the Areopagus and went back to his lodgings. Most of the Greeks were not touched by the good news of Jesus and His love. However, a few people believed, including Dionysius, a member of the council, and a woman named Damaris. This was the only visit Paul made to Athens. A few years later, other apostles established a strong Christian church there, and many Athenians became followers of Jesus.

Paul soon left for Corinth, a city at the crossroads of many travel routes. In Corinth he found a tentmaker named Aquila, and his wife, Priscilla. They were Jewish Christians who had recently come from Rome. Paul was also a tentmaker by trade, and the men became friends and worked together for a while.

Every Sabbath Paul spoke in the synagogue and tried to persuade his listeners that Jesus was the Messiah. He converted both Jews and Greeks. Silas and Timothy were able to come at last from Macedonia and join Paul. At this time, the Holy Spirit prompted Paul to talk to the Jews in Corinth who had not yet heard about Jesus. But when he spoke to them, they argued with him and blasphemed against the name of Jesus. The apostle shook his clothes and said, "Your blood be upon your own

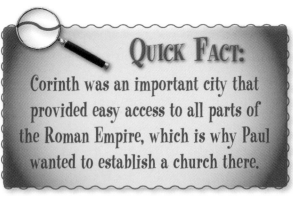

QUICK FACT:
Corinth was an important city that provided easy access to all parts of the Roman Empire, which is why Paul wanted to establish a church there.

heads; I am clean. From now on I will go to the Gentiles."

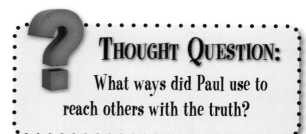

Next, Paul went to the house of Justus, a man who worshiped God and lived next door to a Jewish synagogue. Paul preached in the synagogue on Sabbaths, and many people in Corinth believed and were baptized. The leader of the synagogue, Crispus, and his family came to believe in Jesus. And so the church grew.

One night Paul had a dream, and the Lord spoke to him. "Do not be afraid, but speak, and do not keep silent; for I am with you, and no one will attack you to hurt you; for I have many people in this city."

The three missionaries preached God's message in Corinth for another year and a half. The Jews made an attack on Paul, however, by forcing him to appear before Gallio, the governor of that province. "This fellow," they said, "persuades men to worship God contrary to the law."

Before Paul could speak, the governor said, "If it were a matter of wrongdoing or wicked crimes, O Jews, there would be reason why I should bear with you. But if it is a question of words and names and your own law, look to it yourselves; for I do not want to be a judge of such matters." And he ordered the accusers to leave his courtroom.

Some Greeks of the city had been watching in the court. Outside, the Greeks turned against the men who had accused Paul and beat the ruler of the synagogue. But the governor paid no attention to it.

Paul gained many friends in Corinth, and after three years he said Goodbye to the church members. With Aquila and Priscilla, he sailed to the city of Ephesus, in Syria. Ephesus was a large city. When Paul arrived there he found busy markets and bazaars. There was a lot of trading and shipping from this city to all parts of the Roman Empire. The Jewish citizens of Ephesus received special privileges from the Roman emperor. Because of their religion, Jewish boys were exempted from joining the Roman army.

Paul discussed Jesus and salvation with the Jews in Ephesus for a short time. Then he made plans to continue on to Jerusalem. Leaving Priscilla and Aquila there, he promised them, "I will return again to you, God willing."

TROUBLE IN EPHESUS

Acts 18:22–20:38

Adisciple named Apollos, a Jew from Alexandria, Egypt, came to Ephesus. He had never met Paul, but he preached accurately in the synagogue from the Law and the Prophets. But he only knew about the water baptism of John the Baptist. Aquila and Priscilla heard him speak and invited him to their home. They explained the way of God more fully to him, and he immediately accepted their message. Apollos wanted to travel around the province of Achaia and preach in the towns. With letters of recommendation from the believers in Ephesus, he went on his way across the province. Finally, he ended up in the city of Corinth.

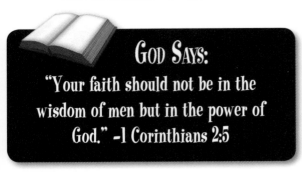

GOD SAYS:
"Your faith should not be in the wisdom of men but in the power of God." -1 Corinthians 2:5

Paul, after attending a religious festival in Jerusalem, had returned to Ephesus. He made that city his headquarters for more than two years. Finding some disciples he had not met before, Paul asked them, "Did you receive the Holy Spirit when you believed?"

"We have not so much as heard whether there is a Holy Spirit," they replied.

"Into what then were you baptized?" Paul asked.

They said, "Into John's baptism."

Paul assured them that John's baptism, which is the baptism of repentance, was good and necessary. But then he laid hands on them and prayed. The Holy Spirit came upon them, and they spoke with tongues and prophesied. There were about twelve men in all.

Paul spent three months preaching about the kingdom of God in the synagogue. However, some of the people hardened their hearts against the message. They began to spread evil and slanderous rumors about the church, now called the Way, and the message of Jesus. Paul decided to withdraw from the synagogue. Taking the believers with him, he studied and preached in a place called the school of Tyrannus.

God worked unusual miracles through Paul among the people of this region. Articles of clothing like aprons and handkerchiefs that had been on Paul's body were taken to sick people, and they were healed. Even those with evil spirits in them were delivered of their oppression by touching these objects.

Some of the idol-worshiping Greeks accepted Jesus and became Christians. They owned books on magic, and they practiced magical arts. But when they became members of the church, the Greeks brought their books and burned them publicly. Someone counted up the value of the materials in one of the bonfires. It was estimated at fifty thousand pieces of silver, a huge sum of money in those days. The apostle Paul was encouraged because God's message spread wonderfully in Ephesus.

A great temple to the Roman goddess Diana, known by the Greeks as Artemis, stood in Ephesus. It was 420 feet long and 220 feet wide, with a double row of marble pillars on each side. It may have been as much as 60 feet tall. This beautiful building was one of the wonders of the ancient world, and worshipers

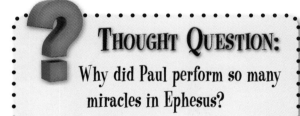

THOUGHT QUESTION: Why did Paul perform so many miracles in Ephesus?

came hundreds of miles to offer sacrifices. Many craftsmen in Ephesus grew wealthy making and selling images of the goddess sitting in a small model of the temple. Some were made of wood and stone, but the most costly were made of silver.

One day a great commotion over Christianity arose in the city's public square. Demetrius, a silversmith, had been making great profit from selling images of Diana. He became upset, however, when he saw many of the people becoming Christians. He gathered all the workers in his trade at the city square and addressed them.

"Men," he said loudly, "you know that we have our prosperity by this trade. Moreover you see and hear that not only at Ephesus, but throughout almost all Asia, this Paul has persuaded and turned away many people, saying that they are not gods which are made with hands. So not only is this trade of ours in danger of falling into disre-

pute, but also the temple of the great goddess Diana may be despised and her magnificence destroyed, whom all Asia and the world worship."

When the workmen heard this they became very angry and cried out, "Great is Diana of the Ephesians!" The commotion spread from the square to the rest of the city, and people rushed to the city amphitheater. Some of the mob seized two of the Christian leaders, Gaius and Aristarchus, and dragged them to the theater also. Paul wanted to appear in front of all the people, but the church members would not allow him.

Most of the crowd in the amphitheater did not even know why they were there. A man named Alexander was pushed to the front to speak, but when word spread that he was Jew, the crowd began to chant, "Great is Diana of the Ephesians!" This went on for about two hours.

Finally, the town clerk quieted the crowd. He told them that the two men they had brought with them were not guilty of robbing temples or

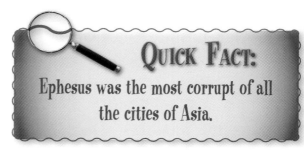

QUICK FACT:
Ephesus was the most corrupt of all the cities of Asia.

speaking blasphemy against their goddess. "Therefore, if Demetrius and his fellow craftsmen have a case against anyone," the clerk announced, "the courts are open and there are proconsuls. Let them bring charges against one another.

"We are in danger," he continued, "of being called in question for today's uproar, there being no reason which we may give to account for this disorderly gathering." After he had said these things, he dismissed the crowd and everyone left.

When the uproar was over, Paul called the church members together and hugged each one of them. Then he said Goodbye and left for Macedonia. He traveled through this region encouraging all the church members. Then he went to Greece, where he stayed for three months. In the meantime, Aquila and Priscilla moved back to Rome to help the church there. Paul loved his two friends, and he once said that they had "risked their own necks for my life."

One thought was uppermost in Paul's mind. He had traveled in many parts of the world, but he had never visited Rome. Someday he hoped to preach the story of Jesus in the capital city of the empire.

Paul traveled on with seven fellow missionaries toward Jerusalem. Stopping at Troas, they held meetings with the church. Since Paul might never see these Christians again, he wanted to spend as much time as he could with them. The day before he was to leave, he spoke to the congregation until midnight.

This meeting was held in a third-story room. A young man named Eutychus, who was sitting on the ledge of an open window, became sleepy as Paul preached longer and longer. Finally, Eutychus was overcome by sleep and fell out of the third-story window. The members rushed downstairs and thought that the young man was dead. But Paul went down, put his arms around Eutychus, and said, "Do not trouble yourselves, for his life is in him." Everyone in the congregation felt great relief.

Back upstairs, Paul ate some bread and continued his talk until daylight. Finally, he left on his journey. By then, Eutychus had recovered and went home very much alive.

Paul and his companions sailed on a boat that did not stop at Ephesus. But he sent for the elders of

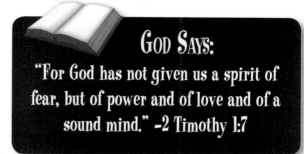

GOD SAYS:
"For God has not given us a spirit of fear, but of power and of love and of a sound mind." –2 Timothy 1:7

that church to meet him at Miletus, a seaport about thirty miles away. When they came, he greeted them warmly and said, "You know, from the first day that I came to Asia, in what manner I always lived among you, serving the Lord with all humility, with many tears and trials which happened to me by the plotting of the Jews; how I kept back nothing that was helpful, but proclaimed it to you, and taught you publicly and from house to house, testifying to Jews, and also to Greeks, repentance toward God and faith toward our Lord Jesus Christ."

The leaders of Ephesus loved Paul, and they listened to his words. "Now I go bound in the spirit to Jerusalem," the apostle continued, "not knowing the things that will happen to me there, except that the Holy Spirit testifies in every city, saying that chains and tribulations await me. But none of these things move me; nor do I count my life dear to myself, so that I may finish my race with joy, and the ministry which I received from the Lord Jesus, to testify to the gospel of the grace of God."

Paul spoke honestly to the leaders, saying, "I know that you all, among whom I have gone preaching the kingdom of God, will see my face no more." This made the elders very sad.

"Therefore take heed to yourselves and to all the flock, among which the Holy Spirit has made you overseers," he encouraged them, "to shepherd the church of God which He purchased with His own blood. For I know this, that after my departure savage wolves will come in among you,

not sparing the flock. Also from among yourselves men will rise up, speaking perverse things, to draw away the disciples after themselves. Therefore watch, and remember that for three years I did not cease to warn everyone night and day with tears.

"So now, brethren," he said in conclusion, "I commend you to God and to the word of His grace, which is able to build you up and give you an inheritance among all those who are sanctified. I have coveted no one's silver or gold or apparel. Yes, you yourselves know that these hands have provided for my necessities, and for those who were with me. I have shown you in every way, by laboring like this, that you must support the weak. And remember the words of the Lord Jesus, that He said, 'It is more blessed to give than to receive.' "

Paul knelt down and prayed with the elders. They cried freely, because they would not see him again. He hugged and kissed each one. When it was time for the apostle to leave, they went with him to the ship and waved a sad farewell.

PAUL IN GREAT DANGER

Acts 21:1–23:11

The ship sailed from the Miletus harbor and headed for the shores of Syria. It stopped a week at Tyre to unload cargo, which gave the apostles time to visit with the Christian believers there. Then the ship set sail again, heading south for Ptolemais. At this port, Paul and his companions were met by members of the church. The next day the group traveled on land to Caesarea, where they were welcomed at the home of Philip the evangelist—the man who had baptized the Ethiopian treasurer. Here they spent a few happy days, the last that Paul was to enjoy in complete freedom.

While the apostles were staying here, a Christian prophet named Agabus came from Judea. Agabus took Paul's belt and bound his own feet and hands with it. Then he said, "Thus says the Holy Spirit, 'So shall the Jews at Jerusalem bind the man who owns this belt, and deliver him into the hands of the Gentiles.'"

When the apostles and the church members heard this, they begged Paul not to go to Jerusalem.

"What do you mean by weeping and breaking my heart?" asked Paul. "I am ready not only to be bound, but also to die at Jerusalem for the name of the Lord Jesus."

Seeing that the warrior of the cross would not yield an inch to their counsel, his companions said, "The will of the Lord be done."

The time came for Paul to go on to Jeru- salem. Besides his fel- low missionaries, some of the disciples from Caesarea went along with him. They made

GOD SAYS:

"For it is better, if it is the will of God, to suffer for doing good than for doing evil." -1 Peter 3:17

the sixty-five miles in a two-day trip, spending the night at the home of a fellow believer.

When the missionary group reached Jerusalem, the church leaders gave them a joyful welcome. The next day Paul had a long talk with James and the other leaders, tell- ing them what God had done in bringing many Gentiles to accept the love of Jesus Christ. He presented gifts of money sent by many of the Gentile churches to help the poor among the Jewish members at Jerusalem.

Although the leaders were happy to hear about Paul's ministry, they also had a problem to solve. Rumors had spread around Judea that Paul had taught Gentile believ- ers to ignore the Law of Moses. Far from ignoring the Law, Paul was a strict adherent. The church leaders sug- gested that Paul join four young men who were perform- ing vows of purification, according to the Law of Moses.

THOUGHT QUESTION:
Why was it important that
Paul keep the Law of Moses?

The apostle could pay the cost of this ceremony, purify himself, and show himself at the temple. They wanted him to do it, they said, "that all may know that those things of which they were informed concerning you are nothing, but that you yourself also walk orderly and keep the law." Paul accepted the suggestion and started to carry out the plan.

The ceremonies took a week to complete, and for several days Paul went in and out of the temple without being noticed. One of the Greeks who had come to Jerusalem with Paul was a young man named Trophimus. The apostle showed him around the city but was very careful not to take him into the temple. No foreigner was allowed beyond the Gentile court on penalty of death.

The week of purification ceremonies was almost over when some Jews from Asia saw Paul in the temple. They assumed that Trophimus the Greek, whom they had now seen with Paul, had come with him into the temple, beyond the Gentile court. These enemies of Jesus began to shout, "Men of Israel, help! This is the man who teaches all men everywhere against the people, the law, and this place; and furthermore he also brought Greeks into the temple and has defiled this holy place."

Of course, the charges were false, but in a short time, people from all over the city were running to the temple.

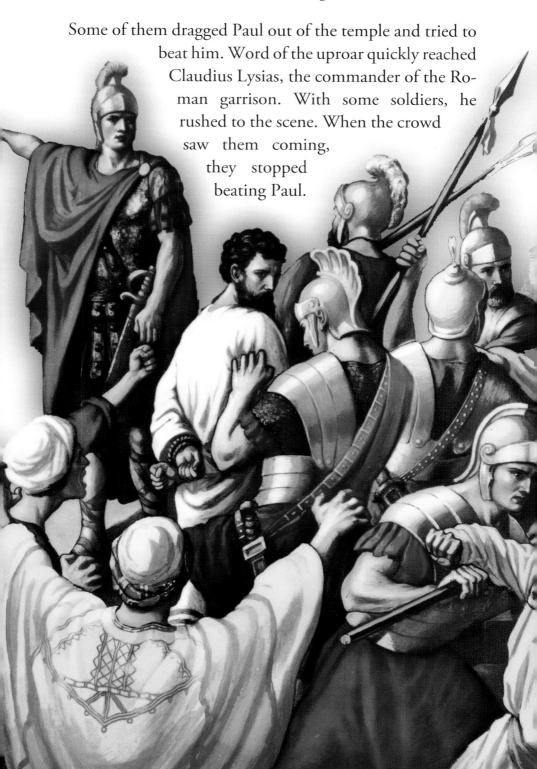

Paul in Great Danger

Some of them dragged Paul out of the temple and tried to beat him. Word of the uproar quickly reached Claudius Lysias, the commander of the Roman garrison. With some soldiers, he rushed to the scene. When the crowd saw them coming, they stopped beating Paul.

The commander had the apostle bound with two chains, and then he asked the crowd what was wrong. Some yelled one thing and some yelled another, so Commander Lysias could not get the facts. At last he ordered Paul to be taken to the barracks. The mob became so violent that the soldiers had to carry Paul the last few meters to the barracks to protect him. The people shouted, "Away with him!"

Just as the soldiers were going to take him into the barracks, Paul turned to the commander and asked, "May I speak to you?"

"Can you speak Greek?" asked Lysias. Not knowing who Paul was, he then asked, "Are you not the Egyptian who some time ago stirred up a rebellion and led the four thousand assassins out into the wilderness?"

"I am a Jew," Paul answered, "from Tarsus, in Cilicia, a citizen of no mean city; and I implore you, permit me to speak to the people."

The commander gave permission, and so Paul stood at the top of the steps and raised his hand toward the crowd. When there was silence, he said, "Brethren and fathers, hear my defense before you now." The crowd became even more quiet when they heard the apostle speak in Hebrew.

He continued, "I am indeed a Jew, born in Tarsus of Cilicia, but brought up in this city at the feet of Gamaliel, taught according to the strictness of our fathers' law, and was zealous toward God as you all are today. I persecuted this Way [the Christian church] to the death, binding and delivering into prisons both men and women, as also the high priest bears me witness, and all the council of the elders, from whom I also received letters to the brethren, and went to Damascus to bring in chains even those who were there to Jerusalem to be punished."

Paul went on to tell how he had heard the voice of Jesus on the road to Damascus when the blaze of light blinded him and that he had accepted Jesus as his Savior and had been baptized. He had returned to Jerusalem but was forced to leave when his life was endangered by enemies. He repeated the message God had given him: " 'Depart, for I will send you far from here to the Gentiles.' "

When the people heard this, they shouted angrily, "Away with such a fellow from the earth, for he is not fit to live!"

As they shouted, men tore off their coats

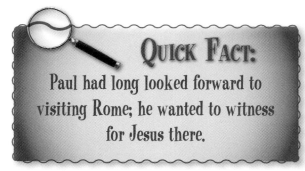

QUICK FACT:
Paul had long looked forward to visiting Rome; he wanted to witness for Jesus there.

and threw dust in the air. The Roman commander ordered the prisoner to be taken into the barracks and whipped, so that he might find out why the people hated Paul so much. When the soldiers had strapped him up and were ready to beat him, Paul asked, "Is it lawful for you to scourge a man who is a Roman, and uncondemned?"

When the commander was told what Paul had said, he came to the prisoner and said, "Tell me, are you a Roman?"

"Yes," said Paul.

"With a large sum I obtained this citizenship," said Lysias, meaning that he had been born a foreigner and purchased his right to be a Roman.

"But I was born a citizen," Paul responded.

The commander was suddenly afraid. He had imprisoned a Roman citizen without having a charge against him. He ordered Paul unbound and sent word to the chief priests and their entire council to meet with him. Some way he had to find out for certain why they hated the apostle. The next day Lysias brought Paul to the meeting and sat him down in front of the Jewish leaders.

Paul looked intently at the council members and said, "Men and brethren, I have lived in all good conscience before God until this day."

Ananias, the high priest, commanded those standing nearest to Paul to strike him in the mouth.

"God will strike you, you whitewashed wall!" Paul cried out. "For you sit to judge me according to the law, and do you command me to be struck contrary to the law?"

Paul noticed at that moment how part of the council was Sadducees and the other part Pharisees. Knowing that the Sadducees did not believe in the resurrection, he called out, "Men and brethren, I am a Pharisee, the son of a Pharisee; concerning the hope and resurrection of the dead I am being judged!"

When the apostle said he was a Pharisee, all the council members who were Pharisees took his side. The Jewish leaders crowded around Paul and got into an argument among themselves, some defending Paul and some accusing him. Finally, the dispute became so loud and violent that the Roman commander was afraid the council members would tear Paul to pieces. He ordered his soldiers to go into the crowd and take Paul from among them by force. Then he sent the prisoner back to the barracks.

Paul must have been confused by this turn of events. But the following night the Lord stood by him and said, "Be of good cheer, Paul; for as you have testified for Me in Jerusalem, so you must also bear witness at Rome." It seemed that the apostle would someday reach the city of Rome after all. He had no idea, however, how he was going to get there.

SAVED FROM A MURDER PLOT

Acts 23:12–24:27

Paul was being held at the Roman barracks in Jerusalem. His Jewish enemies knew they had little chance of killing him while he was in there. The day after Paul's arrest, some of his enemies, more than forty of them, gathered and swore an oath: they would not eat or drink until they had killed Paul.

The plotters went to the chief priests and said, "We have bound ourselves under a great oath that we will eat nothing until we have killed Paul. Now you, therefore, together with the council, suggest to the commander that he be brought down to you tomorrow, as though you were going to make further inquiries concerning him; but we are ready to kill him before he comes near."

Now Paul's sister's son heard about the planned ambush. He hurried to the Roman barracks and told his uncle about it. Paul called a centurion and said to him, "Take this young man to the commander, for he has something to tell him."

The centurion reported that Paul was sending a young man with something to say. Lysias took Paul's nephew by the hand, walked a few steps away from the soldier, and asked him privately, "What is it that you have to tell me?"

QUICK FACT:
God intervened to stop the Jews from killing Paul.

"The Jews have agreed to ask that you bring Paul down to the council tomorrow, as though they were going to inquire more fully about him," the young man replied. "But do not yield to them, for more than forty of them lie in wait for him, men who have bound themselves by an oath that they will neither eat nor drink till they have killed him; and now they are ready, waiting for the promise from you."

Telling the young man not to share this news with anyone else, the commander sent him on his way. Then he called two of his centurions and gave them orders.

"Prepare two hundred soldiers, seventy horsemen, and two hundred spearmen to go to Caesarea at the third hour of the night; and provide mounts to set Paul on, and bring him safely to Felix the governor."

Then Lysias wrote a letter to the governor, telling how the Jews had seized Paul and would have killed him if Roman soldiers had not gone to his rescue. He informed the governor that Paul was a Roman citizen, and because his life was in danger he was sending him to Felix. He also stated that the Jewish accusers had been commanded to present their charges to the governor in person.

In the darkness that night, the guard of Roman soldiers took Paul from the barracks. They rode along the highway northward and reached Caesarea safely. When they came to the governor's residence, Felix read Lysias's letter and then asked Paul where he was from. Hearing that Paul was from Cilicia, he said, "I will hear you when your accusers also have come." The apostle was sent to stay at Herod's old palace.

THOUGHT QUESTION:

What was God's purpose for allowing Paul to be taken before Felix?

Five days later, Ananias the high priest and the Jewish elders arrived with their lawyer, Tertullus, to present their case against Paul. When the lawyer was called upon, he said to the governor, "We have found this man a plague, a creator of dissension among all the Jews throughout the world, and a ringleader of the sect of the Nazarenes. He even tried to profane the temple, and we seized him, and wanted to judge him according to our law. But the commander Lysias came by and with great violence took him out of our hands, commanding his accusers to come to you. By examining him yourself you may ascertain all these things of which we accuse him." There were only vague accusations in the lawyer's pompous speech, because the Jews could not think of a specific charge to make against Paul.

Governor Felix then nodded for Paul to speak. The apostle stood and said, "Inasmuch as I know that you have been for many years a judge of this nation, I do the more cheerfully answer for myself, because you may ascertain that it is no more than twelve days since I went up to Jerusalem to worship. And they neither found me in the temple disputing with anyone nor inciting the crowd, either in the synagogues or in the city. Nor can they prove the things of which they now accuse me."

Paul went on to describe the way he had worshiped in harmony with the Jewish laws. While he was quietly standing in the temple, Jews from Asia had accused him of wrongdoing. Since coming to Jerusalem the apostle said, he had neither incited a riot nor gathered a crowd. He was innocent of any crime against the Jewish religion.

After Felix the governor heard everyone speak, he turned to the Jews and said, "When Lysias the commander comes down, I will make a decision on your case." He ordered the centurion to keep Paul in custody but to allow him some freedom. The officer was not to prevent Paul's friends from visiting him.

God Says:

" 'I myself always strive to have a conscience without offense toward God and men.' " -Acts 24:16

No doubt Philip the evangelist visited Paul and encouraged him during his stay in Herod's palace. Doctor Luke probably came to the apostle and made sure his health was good.

Felix could not forget the words Paul had spoken during the trial. Some days later he and his wife, Drusilla, sent for the apostle. They asked him to explain his faith in Jesus Christ. Now the governor was noted for his evil deeds and crafty political actions. So when Paul talked about goodness and self-control and the time when every man would face the judgment of God, Felix became alarmed. He said to Paul, "Go away for now; when I have a convenient time I will call for you."

Felix hoped that Paul would pay money as a bribe so that he could release him. But the apostle was not a dishonest man. Weeks and months dragged by. When two whole years had passed, Felix was succeeded as governor by Porcius Festus. Felix might have released Paul at any time, because the apostle was guilty of no crime. But the governor had wanted to please the Jews, and he left Paul in custody until the new governor arrived.

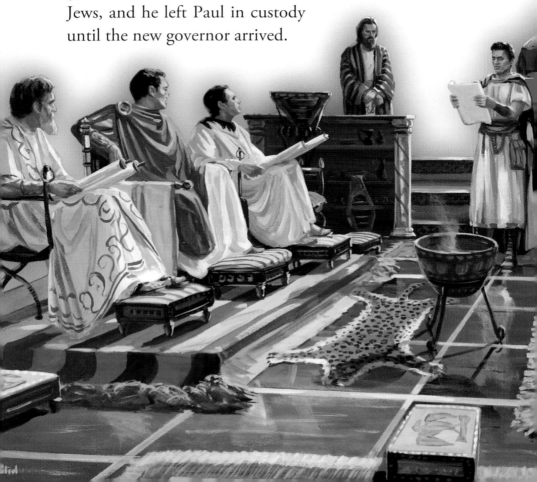

PAUL'S DEFENSE BEFORE A KING

Acts 25; 26

E ven though a long time had passed since the rioting in Jerusalem, the Jews had not forgotten their hatred of Paul. Governor Festus traveled to Jerusalem three days after his arrival in the province. When he arrived, the high priest and the Jewish leaders pressed their charges against the apostle immediately. They begged to have the prisoner sent to Jerusalem, hoping it would give them a chance to kill him.

Festus, however, said Paul should be kept at Caesarea and that he himself was returning there shortly. "Therefore," he said, "let those who have authority among you go down with me and accuse this man, to see if there is any fault in him."

After ten days the governor returned to his palace at Caesarea. The next day he sat in the judgment seat at court and ordered Paul to be brought before him. The Jews who had come from Jerusalem made many serious charges against the apostle. But they had no proof.

GOD SAYS:

" ' "That they may receive forgiveness of sins and an inheritance among those who are sanctified by faith in Me." ' "-Acts 26:18

Then Paul said in his own defense, "Neither against the law of the Jews, nor against the temple, nor against Caesar have I offended in anything at all."

"Are you willing to go up to Jerusalem and there be judged before me concerning these things?" asked Festus. He wanted to do the Jews a favor.

"I stand at Caesar's judgment seat, where I ought to be judged," Paul responded. "To the Jews I have done no wrong, as you very well know. For if I am an offender, or have committed anything deserving of death, I do not object to dying; but if there is nothing in these things of which these men accuse me, no one can deliver me to them. I appeal to Caesar."

After conferring with his council, Governor Festus turned to Paul and said, "You have appealed to Caesar? To Caesar you shall go!"

This meant that the apostle Paul would be taken under guard to Rome. His dream of finally reaching the capital city of the empire would be realized, though not in the way he had imagined. If the Jews wished to press their charges against him, they would now have to go to Rome and appear before the emperor himself.

Some time after this, King Agrippa, the last of the line of Herods, arrived at the palace in Caesarea with his sister, Bernice. After paying their respects to Governor Festus, they stayed on for several days. One day the governor described Paul's case to the king.

"There is a certain man left a prisoner by Felix," the governor began, "about whom the chief priests and the elders of the Jews informed me, when I was in Jerusalem, asking for a judgment against him. . . . Therefore when they had come together, without any delay, . . . I sat on the judgment seat and commanded the man to be brought in. When the accusers stood up, they brought no accusation against him of such things as I supposed, but had some questions against him about their own religion and about a certain Jesus, who had died, whom Paul affirmed to be alive. And because I was uncertain of such questions, I asked whether he was willing to go to Jerusalem and there be judged concerning these matters. But when Paul appealed to be reserved for the decision of Augustus, I commanded him to be kept till I could send him to Caesar."

"I also would like to hear the man myself," said Herod Agrippa.

"Tomorrow," he said, "you shall hear him."

The next day, with great pomp and ceremony, Herod Agrippa and Bernice came into the auditorium attended by officers and leading citizens of Caesarea. Then Paul, his hands and legs fastened with chains, was brought in.

Governor Festus made a short speech to

QUICK FACT:
Festus knew that Paul was innocent but didn't have the courage to set him free.

begin. "King Agrippa and all the men who are here present with us, you see this man about whom the whole assembly of the Jews petitioned me, both at Jerusalem and here, crying out that he was not fit to live any longer. But when I found that he had committed nothing deserving of death, and that he himself had appealed to Augustus, I decided to send him. I have nothing certain to write to my lord [the emperor] concerning

him. Therefore I have brought him out before you, and especially before you, King Agrippa, so that after the examination has taken place I may have something to write. For it seems to me unreasonable to send a prisoner and not to specify the charges against him."

Then King Agrippa said to Paul, "You are permitted to speak for yourself."

In a magnificent speech Paul presented his case to the king. He described how he had been brought up in the Jewish religion and had met Jesus Christ on the road to Damascus. True to the vision, Paul had preached Jesus everywhere he was sent, both in Judea and in the countries of the Gentiles. Finally, to his spellbound listeners he said, "For these reasons the Jews seized me in the temple and tried to kill me. Therefore, having obtained help from God, to this day I stand, witnessing both to small and great, saying no other things than those which the prophets and Moses said would come—that the Christ would suffer, that He would be the first to rise from the dead, and would proclaim light to the Jewish people and to the Gentiles."

At this moment the governor broke in loudly. "Paul, you are beside yourself! Much learning is driving you mad!"

"I am not mad, most noble Festus," said Paul, "but speak the words of truth and reason. For the king, before whom I also speak freely, knows these things; for I am convinced that none of these things escapes his attention, since this thing was not done in a corner. King Agrippa, do you believe the prophets? I know that you do believe."

Agrippa said, "You almost persuade me to become a Christian."

"I would to God that not only you, but also all who hear me today, might become both almost and altogether such as I am, except for these chains," Paul replied. The warrior of the cross held up his shackled arms as he spoke.

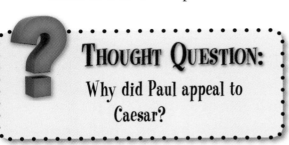

THOUGHT QUESTION:

Why did Paul appeal to Caesar?

Then the king stood, and with the governor and Bernice and those who had sat with him, he left the auditorium. They talked the matter over privately and said, "This man is doing nothing deserving of death or chains."

Then Agrippa said to Festus, "This man might have been set free if he had not appealed to Caesar." What would become of Paul after this meeting, only time could tell.

SHIPWRECKED

Acts 27

Governor Festus decided on a day when Paul and some other prisoners were to start on the long journey to Rome. Along with the apostle went Doctor Luke, his faithful friend, who wrote a full account of their adventures in the book of Acts. Aristarchus, a young Greek Christian from Thessalonica, was permitted to join them.

A centurion of the Augustan regiment named Julius was given charge of the prisoners. The soldiers under his command boarded the captives on a ship bound for ports along the coast of Asia Minor. It was late in the fall of the year, and the prisoners were anxious about the voyage. Small sailing vessels of those days were not safe on stormy seas. This was especially true during the winter months, when fierce hurricanes blasted across the Mediterranean Sea. Sailors steered their ships by one position of the sun and stars, since they had no compass. During storms the sky was covered by clouds for days at a time, and ships lost their way.

Paul's ship arrived safely at the port of Myra. There the centurion Julius found a ship sailing for Italy. He put all the prisoners on board, and they set out to sea once more. For a number of days the ship made slow progress. They sailed south of the island of Crete and with difficulty made their way along the coast until they reached a place called Fair Havens, near the city of Lasea.

Because of the delays, winter was near, and sailing was now dangerous. Paul advised the ship's crew, "Men, I perceive that this voyage will end with disaster and much loss, not only of the cargo and ship, but also our lives."

However, Julius was more influenced by the captain and the helmsman than by Paul. Since that harbor was not suitable to winter in, the majority on the ship favored putting out to sea again. They hoped to reach Phoenix, a harbor on the island of Crete, and spend the winter there.

A light south wind came up, and the crew supposed it was what they needed. They put out to sea and sailed close to Crete. But then a violent head wind called a Northeaster hit them. The ship was caught in the wind and could not face the storm, so the sailors let her run loose before it.

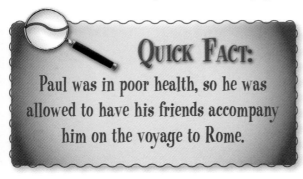

QUICK FACT:
Paul was in poor health, so he was allowed to have his friends accompany him on the voyage to Rome.

The small skiff that was being towed behind the ship, the sailors pulled on board. All the sails were lowered. Some brave sailors dived under the ship from one side to the other with thick ropes, hoping that the cables would hold the ship together. The vessel drifted helplessly, pushed around by huge waves. The next day the ship was tossed up and down so much that the crew threw some of the cargo overboard to lighten it. After three days they dumped the ship's tackle over the side to keep them from sinking.

Many days passed with no sign of the sun or stars, and the storm continued to beat on the ship. Most on board gave up all hope of being saved.

GOD SAYS:

" ' "Do not be afraid, Paul; you must be brought before Caesar; and indeed God has granted you all those who sail with you." ' " –Acts 27:24

Since the beginning of the storm, no one on the ship had eaten anything. Finally, Paul stood up and said, "Men, you should have listened to me, and not have sailed from Crete and incurred this disaster and loss. And now I urge you to take heart, for there will be no loss of life among you, but only of the ship. For there stood by me this night an angel of the God to whom I belong and whom I serve, saying, 'Do not be afraid, Paul; you must be brought before Caesar; and indeed God has granted you all those who sail with you.' Therefore take heart, men, for I believe God that it will be just as it was told me. However, we must run aground on a certain island."

The ship had drifted up and down on the Adriatic Sea. On the fourteenth night, about midnight, the sailors sensed that land was near. Casting a measuring line over the side, they found that they were in shallow water. Now the ship was in danger of being driven by the wind onto the rocks, so they dropped four anchors from the stern. The sailors began to lower the skiff into the water again, under the pretense of releasing anchors at the prow. But they were trying to escape from the ship. Paul saw them and said to the centurion and his soldiers, "Unless these men stay in the ship, you cannot be saved." The Roman soldiers cut the ropes that held the skiff and let it fall off the ship.

Paul urged everyone to eat some food. "Today is the fourteenth day you have waited and continued without food, and eaten nothing," he said. "Therefore I urge you to take nourishment, for this is for your survival, since not a hair will fall from the head of any of you."

Paul then took bread, thanked God for it in front of all the men, and began to eat. All 276 men on the ship then took some food for themselves. When they felt better, the crew threw the last of their cargo of wheat overboard to make the ship as light as possible.

At daybreak the sailors saw a coastline they did not recognize. The captain, seeing a bay with a beach, commanded that the anchors be cut loose. While some sailors loosened the rudder ropes, others hoisted the mainsail, and the ship headed for the beach. But the ship struck a high place on the ocean floor where two strong currents

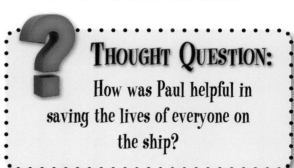

THOUGHT QUESTION:
How was Paul helpful in saving the lives of everyone on the ship?

meet and ran aground. The prow was stuck fast, while large waves struck the stern hard and began to break up the ship.

The Roman soldiers had decided among themselves to kill the prisoners in case any of them should swim away and escape. If any prisoner got away, the soldiers would be executed. But Julius the centurion wanted to save Paul, and he kept the soldiers from killing anyone. He ordered all who could swim to jump overboard and get to land. The others would find a part of the ship to float on.

Paul and the other prisoners, with the crew and the soldiers, jumped into the waves. Their hope was to reach the shore beyond the stormy waters.

PAUL ARRIVES AT ROME

Acts 28

Without the loss of a single prisoner or member of the crew, the 276 shipwrecked men reached the rocky shore. Soon the mariners learned that they had reached the island of Malta. Some men of Malta, who had been watching the stranded ship, welcomed the wet, shivering swimmers. They built a fire on the beach to warm the men, because it was cold and raining.

Paul had gathered a bundle of sticks and put them on the fire. A poisonous snake among the sticks crawled out because of the heat and fastened itself on his hand. Seeing the snake hanging from the apostle's hand, the superstitious Maltese men said, "No doubt this man is a murderer, whom, though he has escaped the sea, yet justice does not allow to live."

Paul shook the creature off into the fire and suffered no harm. However, the men watched him, expecting to see him swell up or fall over dead. After waiting a long time and seeing nothing happen, the men changed their minds and said that Paul must be a god.

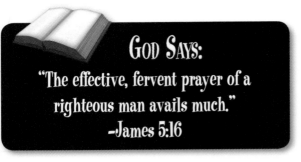

GOD SAYS:
"The effective, fervent prayer of a righteous man avails much."
–James 5:16

Publius, the governor of Malta, lived near the bay. He welcomed the shipwrecked group into his home and entertained them for three days. It happened that the governor's father was sick with a fever and dysentery. Paul went to see him and prayed for him. When the apostle laid his hands on him, the sick man was cured. Soon after, sick people from all parts of the island came to Paul, and he healed them by the power of God. The people of Malta honored Paul and the missionaries with him in many ways.

After three months, the prisoners were taken aboard an Alexandrian ship that had wintered in the harbor. The boat put out and made good headway. After a few days the crew dropped anchor at the harbor of Puteoli, where the prisoners were put ashore. They would travel by road from there to the city of Rome. Some Christians lived in that seaport, and Paul and his companions were allowed to spend a week visiting with them.

As the faithful apostle traveled on toward the emperor's city, some of the Christians from Rome came down to meet him at Appii Forum and Three Inns. When Paul saw these church members, whom he had never met before, he thanked God and felt encouraged.

In Rome, Paul was allowed to live alone in a house with the soldier who guarded him. Three days after he arrived, Paul invited the leading Jews of the city to visit him. When they came to his house, the apostle said, "Men and brethren, though I have done nothing against our people or the customs of our fathers, yet I was delivered as a prisoner from Jerusalem into the hands of the Romans, who, when they had examined me, wanted to let me go, because there was no cause for putting me to death. But when the Jews spoke against it, I was compelled to appeal to Caesar, not that I had anything of which to accuse my nation. For this reason therefore I have called for you, to see you and speak with you, because for the hope of Israel I am bound with this chain."

The leaders replied, "We neither received letters from Judea concerning you, nor have any of the brethren who came reported or spoken any evil of you. But we desire to hear from you what you think; for concerning this sect, we know that it is spoken against everywhere."

They agreed to arrange a meeting for a short time later. On that day a large number of Jews came to Paul's house. They stayed from morning till night while he told the story of Jesus and explained from prophecy that He is the Messiah. Some were convinced that Jesus was the Son of God, but others would not believe. The people left arguing among themselves.

For two years Paul lived in Rome, welcoming everyone who came to visit him. He preached the good news of Jesus openly and unhindered. Many months passed before the Jews from Jerusalem arrived to present their case against Paul to the emperor. During that time the apostle

QUICK FACT:

Although Paul was chained to a soldier at all times, he could come and go as he pleased and live in his own house.

wrote letters of instruction to the Christian churches. Some of these are books of the New Testament, including the letters to the Ephesians, Philippians, and Colossians.

Paul had considerable freedom, but he was probably fastened to a Roman soldier by a light chain attached to his wrist. In one of his letters Paul called himself "an ambassador in chains." To the church at Colossae he wrote that they should pray "also for us, that God would open to us a door for the word, to speak the mystery of Christ, for which I am also in chains, that I may make it manifest" (Col. 4:3, 4).

The companionship of many friends helped keep the prisoner happy. Paul had the help of Aristarchus and Doctor Luke, who had accompanied him on his long voyage from Caesarea. Timothy was in Rome between visits to the churches. Tychicus, a faithful worker, came to the apostle to receive counsel, as did John Mark, Onesimus, and Justus.

Onesimus was an interesting case for Paul to deal with. He was a slave who had run away from his master, Philemon, a Christian believer in Colossae. The runaway servant had gone to Rome, where he heard the good news of Jesus and accepted it. After Paul learned that Onesimus had run away from Philemon and had probably robbed him of money, he told Onesimus that he must return to his master and make everything right.

Paul wrote a letter to Philemon, which is the epistle with that same name in the New Testament. He told Philemon about the servant's change of heart. With compassion he wrote, "I appeal to you for my son Onesimus, whom I have begotten while in my chains, who once was unprofitable to you, but now is profitable to you and to me.

"I am sending him back. You therefore receive him, that is, my own heart, whom I wished to keep with me, that on your behalf he might minister to me in my chains for the gospel. But without your consent I wanted to do nothing, that your good deed might not be by compulsion, as it were, but voluntary" (Philem. 1:10–14).

Paul also asked Philemon to forgive the servant without reservation. He wrote, "If then you count me as a partner, receive him as you would me. But if he has wronged you or owes anything, put that on my account. I, Paul, am writing with my own hand. I will repay—not to mention to you that you owe me even your own self besides" (Philem. 1:17–19). Philemon had come to know Jesus through Paul's preaching.

Paul also had the opportunity to tell the Roman soldiers who guarded him about Jesus of Nazareth. He wrote in one letter, "It has become evident to the whole palace guard,

and to all the rest, that my chains are in Christ" (Phil. 1:13).

The apostle finally appeared before the emperor's court, but his case dragged on for months without a decision. He wrote to the church at Philippi that his troubles were worthwhile. "I want you to know, brethren, that the things which happened to me have actually turned out for the furtherance of the gospel . . . and most of the brethren in the Lord, having become confident by my chains, are much more bold to speak the word without fear" (Phil. 1:12–14).

THOUGHT QUESTION:
Why did God allow Paul to be kept as a prisoner in Rome for so long?

Paul hoped he would soon be released so that he could visit the churches again. He wrote, "I know that this will turn out for my deliverance through your prayer and the supply of the Spirit of Jesus Christ, according to my earnest expectation and hope that in nothing I shall be ashamed, but with all boldness, as always, so now also Christ will be magnified in my body, whether by life or by death" (Phil. 1:19, 20).

During the trial the apostle's close companions must have been absent from Rome. Those who were there who might have helped him were afraid to appear in court. Paul wrote, "At my first defense [in court] no one stood with me, but all forsook me. May it not be charged against them" (2 Tim. 4:16).

The day came, however, when the trial ended and Paul was set free. He thanked God for his liberty and made plans for another missionary journey into Asia Minor.

"I HAVE FOUGHT THE GOOD FIGHT"

Free at last, Paul left Rome to visit the churches. It had been about thirty years since he first met his Master on the road to Damascus. In all of that time, he had never failed in the fight for God's truth.

During the three or four years that Paul remained free this time, he may have preached the good news of Jesus Christ as far west as Spain. He suffered many hardships and went through severe trials in his travels. In a letter to the Corinthian church members, he summed up his adventures:

"From the Jews five times I received forty stripes minus one. Three times I was beaten with rods; once I was stoned;

> **GOD SAYS:**
> "Fight the good fight of faith . . . to which you were also called."
> –1 Timothy 6:12

three times I was shipwrecked; a night and a day I have been in the deep; in journeys often, in perils of waters, in perils of robbers, in perils of my own countrymen, in perils of the Gentiles, in perils in the city, in perils in the wilderness, in perils in the sea, in perils among false brethren; in weariness and toil, in sleeplessness often, in hunger and thirst, in fastings often, in cold and nakedness" (2 Cor. 11:24–27).

Yes, Paul was a true warrior of the cross, a mighty apostle for Jesus Christ!

Finally, his enemies were able to get him arrested and sent to Rome a second time. In the hands of the brutal emperor Nero, the apostle was now made to suffer as a criminal. He was not allowed to live in a house with a guard but was put in the Mamertine Prison and fastened with heavy chains.

Some of the Christians deserted Paul in his darkest hour, but Onesiphorus was faithful and came to the apostle while he was in the dismal dungeon. Doctor Luke stayed on, faithfully caring for his dear friend.

At the trial, Paul must have defended himself in the same strong way he had always fought. He never grew tired of telling how he met Jesus on the road to Damascus and became His follower forever. But now, as he stood before Emperor Nero, his case was hopeless. The godless

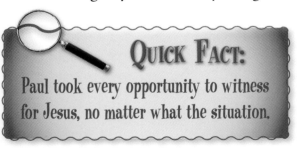

QUICK FACT:
Paul took every opportunity to witness for Jesus, no matter what the situation.

ruler hated the Christians, and he was determined to destroy all of them. At the final trial, Paul was sentenced to die.

In perhaps the last letter he wrote, Paul told Timothy, who was visiting the churches in Asia Minor, to hurry to Rome and bring John Mark with him. Paul knew that his

time was short. "Bring the cloak that I left with Carpus at Troas when you come," he wrote, "and the books, especially the parchments" (2 Tim. 4:13). No doubt the prison was cold, and the aging apostle did not have enough warm clothing for the damp, underground cell.

Paul gave his greatest message of courage in the letter to Timothy when he said, "For I am already being poured out as a drink offering, and the time of my departure is at hand. I have fought the good fight, I have finished the race, I have kept the faith. Finally, there is laid up for me the crown of righteousness, which the Lord, the righteous Judge, will give to me on that Day, and not to me only but also to all who have loved His appearing" (2 Tim. 4:6–8).

In the dim light of the dungeon Paul waited for his dearest friend, Timothy—the youth he had called "son." Whether the young man arrived before the final hour, no one knows. But the apostle was brave and courageous to the last. He had written Timothy, "Do not be ashamed of the testimony of our Lord, nor of me His prisoner" (2 Tim. 1:8).

THOUGHT QUESTION:
What effect did Paul's persecution have on his faith and love for Jesus?

One morning the apostle was taken by Roman soldiers to the place of execution, where the swordsman was waiting. We can be certain that before the moment of death Paul whispered words of faith and hope such as he had written to Timothy: "I have fought the good fight, I have finished the race, I have kept the faith."

FAITHFUL UNTO DEATH

The disciples of Jesus obeyed His instructions to carry the good news of His kingdom to the whole world. At least nine of the disciples went as missionaries, first to the Jews, then to the Roman Empire, and on to more distant countries.

Peter, a man of action, was as anxious to catch men for God as he had once been to catch fish on the Sea of Galilee. The big fisherman was a strong leader in the church. He encouraged new members, telling them about the days he spent with Jesus. When he wrote letters to the churches, he told them about the things he had seen with his own eyes. If they were faithful, they, too, would someday see Jesus face to face.

Near the end of his work, Peter visited the churches in Asia Minor and then made the long journey to Rome. It was while he was in the capital city that Emperor Nero persecuted the Christians. The apostle Peter was one of the first to be put in the Mamertine Prison. He was sentenced to die for his faith. Since he was a Jew and a foreigner, he was to be whipped and then crucified. The big fisherman, remembering how Jesus had been whipped and mocked and nailed to the cross, was ready to follow his Master all the way.

A story has come down to us that as the soldiers were about to nail Peter to the cross, he made a last request. He asked his executioners to crucify him upside down rather than upright. According to this story, the soldiers granted Peter his request, and while he was hanging with his head down and his feet up, he told those who stood nearby how Jesus had died on the cross so that everyone might be saved from sin. Peter still remembered how he had denied Jesus

in a moment of weakness, and he did not feel worthy to be crucified in the same way as his Lord had been. So he died with his head downward.

James, the brother of John, was the first of the apostles to die for his faith. Long before the death of Peter, when persecution of Christian believers raged in Jerusalem, Herod Agrippa, ruler of Galilee, attempted to please the Jewish rulers by putting some of the Christian leaders to death. The apostle James was imprisoned and executed. It was at this time that Peter was put in prison and would have had the same fate if an angel of God had not opened the locked doors and set him free.

James, the brother of Jesus, was one of the leaders in the church at Jerusalem. For years he remained there to guide and direct the council. According to the early church writers, James died a martyr's death in Jerusalem shortly before A.D. 70. His last prayer is said to have been an echo of the Savior's prayer on the cross: "Father, forgive them; for they do not know what they do."

The apostle Thomas is believed to have gone to India as a missionary, and after preaching among the people there, finally to have given his life for the gospel.

Andrew, the brother of Peter, may have preached in Galatia, while Matthew, who had once been a tax collector, went as a missionary to Pontus in Asia Minor.

The apostle Bartholomew may have journeyed to India and on eastward, while Thaddeus is said to have preached in Parthia and ancient Babylon.

These men were not able to tell the good news of Jesus by their own strength. They were given the power of the Holy

Spirit to fulfill the command of Jesus: "Go therefore and make disciples of all the nations, baptizing them in the name of the Father and of the Son and of the Holy Spirit, teaching them to observe all things that I have commanded you" (Matt. 28:19, 20).

Through the centuries, God sent His message of love to the Jewish nation through the prophets, but the leaders refused to obey. Finally, the loving Father sent His only Son, but the nation rejected Him and demanded that He be crucified. The apostles told the good news of Jesus the Messiah first to the Jewish people, and when they rejected it, then to the Gentiles.

On the day Jesus rode triumphantly into the city of Jerusalem on a colt, the people spread their garments in the street and shouted for joy. They thought He was going to free them from the control of the Roman Empire. The Savior looked at the rebellious city and said, "If you had known, even you, especially in this your day, the things that make for your peace! But now they are hidden from your eyes. For days will come upon you when your enemies will build an embankment around you, surround you and close you in on every side, and level you, and your children within you, to the ground; and they will not leave in you one stone upon another, because you did not know the time of your visitation" (Luke 19:42–44).

GOD SAYS:

"Watch, stand fast in the faith, be brave, be strong." –1 Corinthians 16:13

Jesus warned His followers about this time when enemy

armies would attack Jerusalem and make it impossible for anyone to escape. The Master declared, "But when you see Jerusalem surrounded by armies, then know that its desolation is near. Then let those who are in Judea flee to the mountains, let those who are in the midst of her depart, and let not those who are in the country enter her. For these are the days of vengeance, that all things which are written may be fulfilled. But woe to those who are pregnant and to those who are nursing babies in those days! For there will be great distress in the land and wrath upon this people. And they will fall by the edge of the sword, and be led away captive into all nations. And Jerusalem will be trampled by Gentiles until the times of the Gentiles are fulfilled" (Luke 21:20–24).

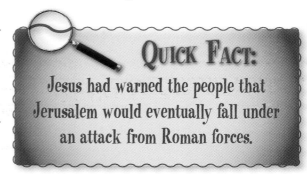

QUICK FACT:
Jesus had warned the people that Jerusalem would eventually fall under an attack from Roman forces.

During the years that the Christian church was growing under the leadership of Peter, Paul, and the other apostles, many zealous Jews made preparations to rise against their Roman rulers to gain freedom. In A.D. 66, the rebels attacked the Roman forces in Jerusalem. When Emperor Nero heard of this, he sent his famous general, Vespasian, to end the strife. The rebellion continued, however. When Nero died, Vespasian was called to Rome to be emperor. He left his son, Titus, to lead an army of eighty thousand soldiers against the walled city of Jerusalem.

The Jews would not surrender, and those who tried to

escape were crucified on crosses outside the city. Famine struck the helpless citizens, and tens of thousands died. The people starved to death rather than surrender. In July, A.D. 70, those guarding the castle of Antonia were surprised and overtaken at night. The Roman army now entered Jerusalem with ease.

General Titus intended to save the magnificent temple, but the historian Josephus tells us what happened. He says, "Then a certain soldier took a flaming firebrand and cast it into the golden gate, which entered into the rooms on the north part of the temple.

"News was brought to Titus, and he rushed into the temple to hinder the fire, taking his captains with him. With voice and hand he tried to signal the soldiers, but they could not be restrained either by command or threatenings, but everyone went where fury carried him, and thronging together at the entrance many pressed one another to death, and many amongst the flaming ruins of the galleries perished.

"When they came to the temple itself, they pretended not to hear Titus, and the Caesar could not restrain the fury of the madbrained soldiers, and the fire increased.

"So Titus entered into the temple with his nobles, and saw all the holy things, far surpassing any description and report that had been given of them.

"The flames, not having passed into the inner part of the temple, nor yet consumed the houses and rooms about it, Titus thought it might even yet be preserved. Therefore he came forward and entreated the soldiers to extinguish the fire, and commanded the centurion of his guard to

beat back the soldiers with his truncheon. But their fury and rage of war, and the hatred they bore against the Jews, overcame all fear of commands. Many hoped for booty, thinking that all the temple was full of money.

"Then a certain soldier fired the posts above the doors, and when Titus saw the flames within he went away.

"It was now hopeless, and everyone stood looking on without trying to extinguish the flames.

"Thus the temple was burned down against the will of Titus."

Jesus had told His disciples that the temple buildings would lie in utter ruin. He said, "These things which you see—the days will come in which not one stone shall be left upon another that shall not be thrown down" (Luke 21:6). The gold from the temple

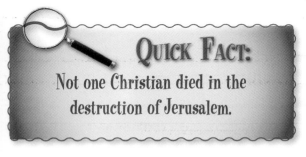

QUICK FACT:
Not one Christian died in the destruction of Jerusalem.

melted in the fire and ran down between the stones so that the soldiers actually tore them up to find the treasure.

Jerusalem had been completely destroyed. What happened to the Christians? They had remembered the words of Jesus, and before the Roman armies surrounded Jerusalem, they left the city and went to the town of Pella, east of the Jordan River. History records that not one Christian died in the terrible war and destruction.

Jesus loved His people in Israel, but they rejected Him. He said, "O Jerusalem, Jerusalem, the one who kills the prophets and stones those who are sent to her! How often I wanted to gather your children together, as a hen gathers her chicks under her wings, but you were not willing! See! Your house is left to you desolate; for I say to you, you shall see Me no more" (Matt. 23:37–39).

A LONELY EXILE SEES HEAVEN

1 John; 2 John; 3 John; Revelation

Johntext ohn, the son of Zebedee and youngest of the twelve disciples of Jesus, was an old man past ninety years of age. He had faithfully told the good news of his Master for many years. Now the apostle was on the lonely, rocky island of Patmos, where he had been banished by Emperor Domitian. This tiny island is in the storm-tossed Aegean Sea, southwest of Ephesus.

As the apostle John walked on this desolate island, he thought back on his life. He was the last of the twelve men who had been close to Jesus. The others had all died. John remembered how he had loved to be with his Master. He, among all the friends of the Savior, had been called "the disciple whom [Jesus] loved."

The aged man thought back to the day when Jesus walked by him on the shore of the Sea of Galilee. John and his brother, James, were in fishing boats, helping their father mend nets, when Jesus called the two young men. When He invited them to follow Him, they had immediately left their work and gone with the Man of Nazareth. John was probably under twenty years of age when he became a disciple, and now, more than a half century later, he could say he had never forgotten his call.

The old man smiled as he remembered being one of the three disciples who were with Jesus on special occasions. John was with James and Peter when his Lord was transfigured on the Mount of Olives. He was also nearby in the darkness when Jesus prayed in the Garden of Gethsemane.

As John looked out over the restless waters of the Aegean Sea, he remembered the day Jesus died.

The young man was standing near the cross, comforting Mary, the mother of Jesus,

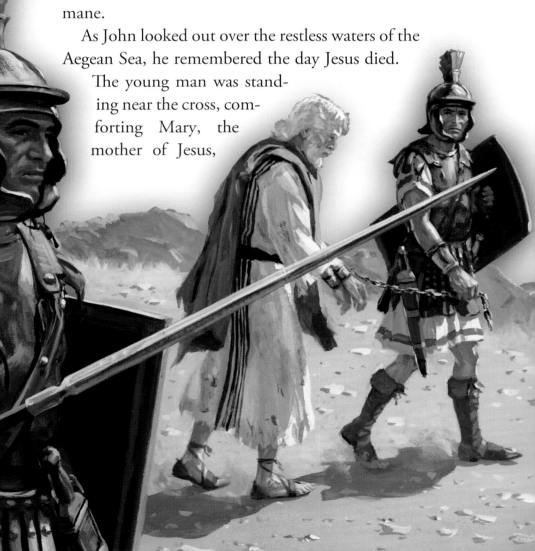

when the dying Man spoke. Jesus had said to Mary, "Woman, behold your son!" And to John, the Crucified One had gasped, "Behold your mother!" (John 19:26, 27).

Yes, John had obeyed the request of the Master, because he had cared for Mary as if she were his own mother.

John bowed his head as he thought of the foolish things he and James had done to hurt Jesus. One day when they had gone to a village in Samaria, the people had rejected Him. This made the two disciples angry, and they said that fire should come down from heaven and destroy the ungrateful men and women. But the Savior had showed the disciples that they did not yet have His love in their hearts.

Again, John remembered how he and his brother had tried to get the most important jobs in the kingdom they expected Jesus to establish. Their mother had gone with them to ask for the highest honors. Now the aged apostle shook his head as he thought of his selfishness and how disappointed Jesus had looked when He heard their requests.

John loved his Master, and he had never stopped telling the story of God's love. To the churches he

God Says:

"Behold what manner of love the Father has bestowed on us, that we should be called children of God!" -1 John 3:1

had written these words: "Beloved, let us love one another, for love is of God; and everyone who loves is born of God and knows God. He who does not love does not know God, for God is love. In this the love of God was manifested toward us, that God has sent His only begotten Son into the world, that we might live through Him" (1 John 4:7–9).

The exiled man on Patmos island remembered the years after Jesus had returned to heaven. Peter was his close friend. The two men had worked to make the church strong. John thought of the day they had healed the lame man at the temple gate. He remembered, too, the trip he made to Samaria with Peter to help settle some church problems. But the apostle Peter was gone. Paul was gone. James was gone. John was the last disciple left.

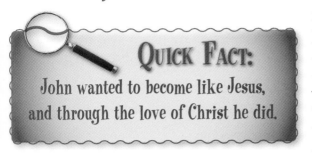

QUICK FACT:
John wanted to become like Jesus, and through the love of Christ he did.

He thought, too, of his work among the churches. He had been a preacher of the Cross until the day the soldiers took him to Rome to stand before the emperor. When the ruler could not frighten this courageous apostle, he sentenced him to be thrown into a large tank of boiling oil. But God saved the life of His faithful servant, just as He had protected the three young men in Nebuchadnezzar's fiery furnace.

When John could not be killed in this way, the emperor decreed that he should be sent into exile on Patmos island. With no regret John could write to his friends, saying, "That which was from the beginning, which we have heard, which we have seen with our eyes, which we have looked upon, and our hands have handled, concerning the

Word of life—the life was manifested, and we have seen, and bear witness . . . and truly our fellowship is with the Father and with His Son Jesus Christ" (1 John 1:1–3).

John knew that many of the Christians were in prison or had been tortured, burned, torn to pieces by wild animals, or exiled. But in his letters the apostle encouraged the church members to be faithful, giving them this precious promise from Jesus: " ' "Hold fast what you have, that no one may take your crown. He who overcomes, I will make him a pillar in the temple of My God, and he shall go out no more" ' " (Rev. 3:11, 12).

It was on this lonely island that John wrote Revelation, the last book in the Bible. As he began to write to the churches, he explained where he was and why he was a prisoner. "I, John, both your brother and companion in the tribulation and kingdom and patience of Jesus Christ, was on the island that is called Patmos for the word of God and for the testimony of Jesus Christ" (Rev. 1:9).

While in exile, John was given the wonderful vision of what God is preparing for all those who are true to Him. He saw the glorious prize that awaits the true followers of the Cross who have fought the good fight. The apostle wrote these words describing our wonderful home: "Now I saw a new heaven and a new

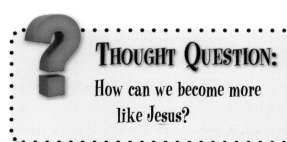

THOUGHT QUESTION:
How can we become more like Jesus?

earth, for the first heaven and the first earth had passed away. Also there was no more sea. Then I, John, saw the holy city, New Jerusalem, coming down out of heaven from God, prepared as a bride adorned for her husband. And I heard a loud voice from heaven saying, 'Behold, the tabernacle of God is with men, and He will dwell with them, and they shall be His people. God Himself will be with them and be their God. And God will wipe away every tear from their eyes; there shall be no more death, nor sorrow, nor crying. There shall be no more pain, for the former things have passed away' " (Rev. 21:1–4).

Describing the city he saw, John wrote, "[An angel] carried me away in the Spirit to a great and high mountain, and showed me the great city,

the holy Jerusalem, descending out of heaven from God, having the glory of God. Her light was like a most precious stone, like a jasper stone, clear as crystal. Also she had a great and high wall with twelve gates, and twelve angels at the gates, and names written on them, which are the names of the twelve tribes of the children of Israel. . . .

"The city had no need of the sun or of the moon to shine in it, for the glory of God illuminated it. The Lamb is its light. And the nations of those who are saved shall walk in its light, and the kings of the earth bring their glory and honor into it. . . .

"And he showed me a pure river of water of life, clear as crystal, proceeding from the throne of God and of the Lamb. In the middle of its street, and on either side of the river, was the tree of life, which bore twelve fruits, each tree yielding its fruit every month. The leaves of the tree were for the healing of the nations. And there shall be no more curse. . . . There shall be no night there: They need no lamp nor light of the sun, for the Lord God gives them light. And they shall reign forever and ever" (Rev. 21:10–22:5).

What a beautiful home God is preparing for us! We have had pain and heartaches here, but in the new earth that will all be in the past. And, best of all, we will see our Friend, Jesus Christ, face to face.

Don't you want to be there?

TRUE TO THEIR CAPTAIN

As the Christian church grew, the followers of Jesus were persecuted by the pagan rulers of the Roman Empire. In order to punish these honest men and women, it was necessary to accuse them of evil deeds. They were charged with bringing terrible calamities, such as fires, famines, plagues, and earthquakes, upon the empire.

The city of Rome caught fire during the reign of Emperor Nero. For nine days the fire burned, and two-thirds of the great city was destroyed. The emperor blamed the Christians for the disaster and ordered them to be put to death. He devised some of the most cruel tortures possible. Some of the Christians were covered with the skins of wild animals and left to be mangled and eaten by wild dogs.

> ## GOD SAYS:
> " 'Blessed are those who are persecuted for righteousness' sake, for theirs is the kingdom of heaven.' "
> –Matthew 5:10

Others were nailed to crosses, while some were covered with tar and burned as torches in the night. The emperor offered his own garden for that occasion, and he held a chariot race to make the party more exciting.

However, we would expect the Roman rulers to hate the followers of Jesus Christ. After all, the church members refused to worship the emperor as a god, and they would not take part in the sacrifices made to idols. Nor would they burn incense on pagan altars.

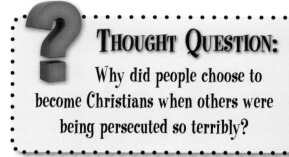

THOUGHT QUESTION:
Why did people choose to become Christians when others were being persecuted so terribly?

Among the Christians who died as heroes of the cross, there was Ponticus, a boy of fifteen, who endured suffering and death for his Savior. There was a slave girl, Blandina, who was tortured to force her to give up her faith in Jesus. She was thrown to wild animals in the gladiator's arena, but when a hungry lion was let loose upon the poor child, she looked into his mouth and smiled like a queen. The lion did not touch her. Some said that the brightest page in the history of Rome was written that day, in the beams of that child's hope.

The greatest of all persecutions against the Christians came two hundred years after the death of the apostle John during the reign of the emperor Diocletian. Church buildings were destroyed, and thousands of Christians were put to death by the sword, killed by wild animals, or executed by burning.

Many of the followers of Jesus Christ were hunted like animals, and one historian says that the tombs in Rome gave shelter for thousands. "Beneath the hills outside the city of Rome, long galleries had been tunneled through earth and rock; the dark and intricate network of passages extended for miles beyond the city walls. In these underground retreats, the followers of Christ buried their dead; and here also, when suspected and proscribed, they found a home."

Graves were cut into the rock. After the dead were buried, the tomb was closed with a slab of marble or tile. On these slabs, explorers have found inscriptions that tell of the hope of the Christians. The church members knew that Jesus was the Resurrection and the Life, and they looked forward to the day when they would see their loved ones again.

When the love of Jesus entered the hearts of men and women, they stood true to Him in time of suf-

fering and death. They remembered the words of Jesus: "He who loves father or mother more than Me is not worthy of Me" (Matt. 10:37). Men and women of all classes— nobles and senators and rich merchants, mothers and their daughters, the old and the young—endured persecution and death because of their faith.

As the pagan Romans saw the courage of the Christians, they were led to ask, "What is the faith of these people that makes them willing to die for their Lord?" It was not long before thousands of them wanted to hear the story of Jesus, and many followed the way of eternal life. Thus, the blood of the Christian martyrs became the seed from which the church grew.

HOLD HIGH THE TORCH

In ancient times, Greek athletes ran races in which they carried a torch of "sacred fire" from the pagan temple to a faraway city. The first man lit his torch at the altar, where the flame was always kept burning. He carried it along the highway, over hills, and through valleys, to the next runner, who was waiting to snatch the torch from the first runner and race on toward the finish. Thus, the fire was carried from one place to another.

In a similar way, men and women who loved Jesus Christ took the torch of truth from the hands of the apostles and carried it to others. They passed it to the next generation of faithful Christians, and in this way the story of Jesus was carried to the world.

Among the early runners who carried the torch for Jesus was Clement, a leader in the church, who had been taught by Peter and Paul. He may have been the "fellow worker" whom Paul mentions in his letter to the Philippians. Clement was a Roman from a distinguished family. He instructed the church members to love God and people and to be humble and holy. By his life and his deeds, Clement followed in the footsteps of his Master.

Ignatius was a Christian who took care of the church at Antioch in Syria. Because of his courage in preaching the story of Jesus, he was condemned to death by the emperor Trajan. He was taken to Rome to be thrown to wild animals in the Colosseum. On the way, he wrote letters to some of the churches, urging them to be faithful. He wrote about his journey in these words: "From Syria to Rome I fight with wild beasts, on water and on land, by day and by night, chained to ten leopards [soldiers]. . . . Would that I might be glad of the beasts made ready for me. And I

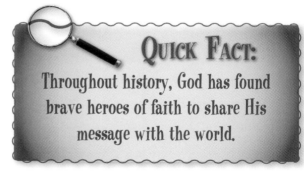

QUICK FACT:
Throughout history, God has found brave heroes of faith to share His message with the world.

pray that they may be found ready for me. Nay, I will fawn upon them, that they may devour me quickly, and not, as they have done with some, refuse to touch me from fear. Yea, and if they will not voluntarily do it, I will bring them to it by force."

Another leader of the church of Antioch, who followed Ignatius, was Polycarp. He was a sincere and humble man who never felt equal to the apostles. He wrote to the church at Philippi, saying, "Neither I, nor any other like me, can attain the wisdom of the blessed and glorious

Paul, who was among you; . . . who also in his absence wrote you an epistle, from which ye may edify yourselves in the faith given to you." He urged the church members to love God and Jesus Christ and to be kind to their neighbors.

Polycarp was brought before the Roman rulers in A.D. 155 and condemned to die by burning at the stake. The soldiers were supposed to tie him up, but he assured them that he would not try to get away. He said, "I shall abide and not stir in the midst of the fire." He died with these courageous words on his lips: "Let us then, if we suffer for His name's sake, glorify Him, for He has set us the example in Himself, and we have believed."

As the centuries passed, the story of Jesus spread from country to country. The torch of truth burned bright, although enemies sometimes tried to put out the flame. In the foothills of the Alps in Italy, a man named Peter Waldo taught the love of Jesus. The people who accepted the message that he preached were called Waldenses. The children in these families were taught to read and write, and they also studied the Bible. From the schools, young men went out as missionaries to spread the word about Jesus. Sometimes they went disguised as peddlers to the castles and homes of the rich. After showing expensive goods and jewels, they would bring out the Bible and tell the story of Jesus. Enemies of the truth persecuted the Waldenses, and armies came to destroy the faithful men, women, and children. But God protected His people. Many of them found refuge in caves and other secret places in the mountains.

Other men of God carried the torch of truth in England. A young college student named John Wycliffe read the Bible and loved its message.

"I resolve to profess and defend the law of Christ as long as I have power," he declared.

The people could not read the Scriptures in those days, because they were written only in Latin. Young Wycliffe determined to translate the Bible into English so that ordinary citizens could read it for themselves. He spent from ten to fifteen years translating the Bible. Copies were written by hand, because this was before the days of printing. Although enemies tried to stop the work of Wycliffe by burning many of the Bibles, the torch of truth could not be put out.

THOUGHT QUESTION:

How can God help us stay strong when we are persecuted for our faith?

Another Englishman who loved the Bible was John Tyndale. Like Wycliffe, he was determined to see that the Word of God was placed in the homes of the people. To some of the church leaders who tried to stop his work, he said, "If God spares my life, I will take care that a plowboy shall know more of the Scriptures than you do."

Tyndale worked long and hard at his translation. Sometimes he was hungry and cold, because he had little money. At last the Bible was ready. It could now be printed rather than copied, and Tyndale went to Europe to have the work done. After meeting great difficulties, he saw copies of the Scriptures ready to ship to England. The books were sold secretly. Many students of Oxford University, the leading university of England, obtained God's Word for themselves. Enemies tried to burn the Bibles and stop Tyndale's work, but the torch of truth could not be put out.

As the church became bigger and more powerful through the centuries, many forgot the teachings of Jesus. In Germany, a young priest named Martin Luther longed to see a revival of God's truth in the church. At the university library he found a complete Bible and began to read it. Up to this time, he had seen only parts of the Scriptures, such as the four Gospels. As he read the wonderful words, he exclaimed, "Oh, that God would give me such a Book for myself!"

Luther began to write and to preach. He told church members that Jesus died to forgive all their sins and that anyone could be saved by having faith in God. Enemies of this truth opposed Martin Luther, and he was brought to trial. He was asked to give up his beliefs, but the soldier of the cross stood firm. He said, "Unless, therefore, I am convinced by the testimony of Scripture, or on plain and clear grounds of reason, so that conscience shall bind me to make acknowledgement of error, I can and will not retract." Then he looked at his accusers and declared, "Here I stand. I can do no other. May God help me. Amen."

Martin Luther translated the Bible into German so that his people might read it. He composed the well-known church hymn, "A Mighty Fortress Is Our God," and as a carrier of the torch of truth he led thousands of men and women to find the love of Jesus.

In France, there was a faithful Christian named John Calvin. As he read the Bible, he found peace in his heart.

He went forth with the torch of truth to show others the way to heaven.

John Knox of Scotland was a courageous witness for the faith of Jesus. Twice he was expelled from his homeland as an exile because of his preaching. However, he was not afraid to stand before the queen of Scotland and preach the truth. She was stunned, amazed, and speechless at what she heard. Knox pleaded with her to obey God's Word. He said, "I pray God, madam, that ye may be as blessed within the commonwealth of Scotland as ever was Deborah in the commonwealth of Israel."

Bravely John Knox followed his Master. "With ceaseless energy and unfaltering courage he kindled a spark wherever he went, till the light burst out all over the land."

145

More than a century later, two upright men of England gave their hearts to Christ. John and Charles Wesley were brothers who helped thousands of the poor working people of England by making the teachings of Jesus so simple and practical that anyone could understand and follow them. In hours of darkness and trouble, the Wesleys trusted in God. The brothers wrote many hymns of praise that are sung to this day. As a result of their service to God, the Methodist Church was founded.

GOD SAYS:

" 'And God will wipe away every tear from their eyes; there shall be no more death, nor sorrow, nor crying.' "–Revelation 21:4

In the early 1800s, a man in America studied God's Word and went to his friends and neighbors with the message that Jesus was coming back to earth very soon. He was William Miller of New England. He believed the prophecies of the Bible and preached Christ's promise, "I will come again." Called by God to preach, William Miller shared the message with thousands of people, and many believed it.

About this time, Christians began going from Europe to faraway countries to preach the gospel. One of the first to leave home and friends was William Carey. He said, "My business is preaching the gospel; I cobble shoes to pay expenses." In 1792, he sailed for India as a missionary. Christians back in his homeland gave money to help pay his expenses. He said, "I will venture to go down, but remember that you must hold the ropes."

Carey was a pioneer in India. He worked in a factory, preached in villages, translated the Bible, and printed the Scriptures in one of the native languages. Before he died in 1834, this carrier of the torch saw other missionaries go to China, Burma, Africa, and the South Sea Islands. Dr. David Livingstone went into the jungles and savannahs of Africa to care for the sick and tell them about Jesus. John Williams became a missionary to the cannibals of the South Sea Islands. Adoniram Judson was "the apostle to Burma," while Robert Morrison spent years in China pioneering the way for the gospel.

Today, there are thousands of missionaries who have left their homes and friends to carry the story of Jesus. They go to huge cities filled with people and isolated villages in remote regions of the world. We hold the torch of Jesus Christ also, in our homes, in school, and at work and play. Jesus says, "Follow Me." He longs for friends who are loyal and true to Him. He loves you and comes knocking on the door of your heart today.

INDEX OF TOPICS
PRESENTED IN THESE
CHARACTER-BUILDING STORIES

Index of Topics

Faith/Trust

Giving/Unselfishness

Helping Others

Index of Topics

Kindness

Learning to Forgive

Love for Others

Obedience

Index of Topics

Prayer Answered

The Search for a Bride
1:85

Elijah, Fighter for God
3:65

Elisha Captures an Army
3:88

Daniel in the Den of Lions
3:134

Peter, Champion of Truth
5:38

Self-control

A Slave in Prison
1:127

Samson Wants His Own Way
2:126

David and His Mighty Men
3:32

Saved From a Murder Plot
5:91

Worship of God

When Cain Hated His Brother
1:29

When God Spoke From the Mountain
2:45